The Balance Gap

The Balance Gap

Working Mothers and the Limits of the Law

Sarah Cote Hampson

Stanford Law Books
An Imprint of Stanford University Press
Stanford, California

Stanford University Press
Stanford, California

Printed in the United States of America on acid-free, archival-quality paper

Library of Congress Cataloging-in-Publication Data

Names: Hampson, Sarah Cote, author.
Title: The balance gap : working mothers and the limits of the law / Sarah Cote Hampson.
Description: Stanford, California : Stanford Law Books, an imprint of Stanford University Press, 2017. | Includes bibliographical references and index.
Identifiers: LCCN 2016037521 (print) | LCCN 2016038326 (ebook) | ISBN 9781503600058 (cloth : alk. paper) | ISBN 9781503602151 (pbk. : alk. paper) | ISBN 9781503602175
Subjects: LCSH: Mothers—Employment—Law and legislation—United States. | Working mothers—Legal status, laws, etc.—United States. | Work and family—United States. | Women college teachers—Legal status, laws, etc.—United States. | United States—Armed Forces—Women—Legal status, laws, etc.
Classification: LCC KF3555 .H36 2017 (print) | LCC KF3555 (ebook) | DDC 344.7301/44—dc23
LC record available at https://lccn.loc.gov/2016037521

For Chris, Anna, and Elisabeth

Acknowledgments

This book represents the culmination of years of hard work, but also decades of dreaming that one day I would write a book. I owe so much to the many who have supported me in writing it.

Many thanks to Michelle Lipinski and the anonymous reviewers at Stanford University Press, whose feedback has improved this book tremendously. Special thanks to Renee Cramer, who provided feedback on the manuscript at an early stage and saw enough promise in it to recommend that Michelle read it. I will always be grateful for your mentorship and support!

Thanks as well to Kristin Kelly, Jeff Dudas, and Virginia Hettinger, who served on my dissertation committee and whose support and insights on this project during its developmental stages were absolutely invaluable. Thank you to Evelyn Simien and Heather Turcotte, who served as readers on the dissertation and have always offered me their support and guidance.

I am forever indebted to my writing group from graduate school—Jamie Huff, Daniel Tagliarina, and Alexander Reger—without whose help in the early stages of this project this book most certainly would never have been finished and whose friendship and feedback I value so much. Special thanks to honorary writing group member Allyson Yankle, my own personal Google Alert for all things work/life balance. I am also grateful for the help and feedback of my colleagues during the development of the book proposal—Turan Kayaoglu, Ellen Bayer, and Elizabeth

Bruch—and others at the University of Washington Tacoma who write with me and encourage me.

Thank you to all of the brave, anonymous women who came forward to participate in this research. I am inspired by all of your stories, and thinking of you often kept me working when the going got tough on this project.

Finally, and most of all, I thank my family. My parents, Dan and Penny Cote, always believed in me and told me I could do anything. Thanks to Barbara, Martin, Seth, and Rachel—all of whom have offered me support on this project in one way or another. The biggest thanks go to my husband, Christopher Hampson, my rock who does so much of the invisible work that makes things like writing a book while raising a family possible. I also thank my daughters, Anna and Elisabeth, for teaching me firsthand about the struggles of work/life balance. I want nothing more than for this journey to be an easier one for you.

Contents

Introduction: In Pursuit of "Balance"

Natalie is an active-duty major in the U.S. Air Force. Achieving her rank after twelve years of service, Natalie describes herself as "competitive" in her career. She is also a mother of two young children. When it comes to having children in her line of work, Natalie says she talks about her family life with many of her peers but avoids mentioning to her supervisor that she is a mother. "I don't want people to think that the number of my children or my family life keeps me from being able to do my job. I don't want, for instance, for that to be held against me that I wouldn't be able to do a job."

Yet that is exactly what Natalie says happened to her when she interviewed for a "pretty big job" after having her second child: "I had to prove that I had a nanny for my children and that it wouldn't interfere with my job." The job would require a lot of travel, she explains, and the woman interviewing her had expressed concern for Natalie's ability to balance family with such a demanding professional role. In the end, Natalie didn't get the job. "I mean . . . now I can see why I probably didn't need the job, but at the time, and still, you feel a little . . . that because you have children that's being held against you. To me, I want you to look at my record and if my record speaks for itself, then you should hire me, and I'll take care of my family . . . because honestly most men when they go interview for a job, they're not asked how many kids do you have and who's going to be taking care of them." Still, Natalie says she "struggles" to find "the right jobs to further my career. . . . I don't want to hurt my family in doing so." Natalie says that she is trying to find a balance between her work and her family life that is proving elusive. "I think about that quite often. I'm trying to find that perfect—well, there's no such thing as perfect—but trying to find that equal ground with both of them [work and family]."

Can women "have it all"? Can women ever truly find a "balance" between work and family? Natalie is not alone among working mothers in America wondering whether she can ever find a way to successfully integrate the domestic and professional facets of her life. Successful women such as Facebook chief operating officer Sheryl Sandberg and former director of policy planning for the U.S. State Department Ann Marie Slaughter have recently weighed in on these questions in prominent media outlets. While this is certainly not the first time Americans have engaged in national discussions about women and work, renewed attention to the tensions between work and family are to be found everywhere, from the pages of the *New York Times*[1] to John Oliver's HBO news comedy show, *Last Week Tonight*,[2] and, most recently, in the campaign rhetoric of both major party nominees in the 2016 presidential election.[3]

This public discourse simply mirrors what many women such as Natalie are experiencing as a daily reality. Women feel frustrated by a lack of options for paid leave, high-quality, low-cost child care, and entrenched cultural expectations that converge to create significant barriers to their success in the workplace.

In recent decades, laws and workplace policies have emerged that aim to address some of these problems. Millions of women in the United States take some time off when they give birth or adopt a child using "family-friendly" laws and policies in order to spend time recuperating and to initiate a bond with their children. Such allowances are grounded in federal law (the Family and Medical Leave Act of 1992), state and municipal laws (e.g., California's Paid Family Leave Law of 2002 or the city of Seattle's

2015 introduction of paid parental leave for city employees), and individual institutional policies. In recent years, another wave of policies aimed at improving the rate of breast-feeding among working mothers has also taken hold throughout various states. A provision in the Affordable Care Act has brought similar accommodation requirements through federal law, and many workplaces have indeed gone above and beyond state and federal requirements and implemented multiple lactation rooms and on-site support services.

Policies that aim to improve work/life balance are often created with the hope that changes in structural support for women in the workplace will foster social changes to also take effect at work. Activists and policymakers hope that such policy changes will not only increase women's participation in the workplace but also help women to experience greater overall equity as workers. These policies, however, have thus far fallen short of fully alleviating the tensions that women across the nation are still grappling with as they try to balance their work and their family responsibilities. A recent Pew Research Center survey shows, for instance, that mothers are still far more likely to experience a career interruption than fathers in order to fulfill caregiving work. The study notes that 42 percent of mothers have reduced their working hours in order to care for a child or family member, compared with 28 percent of men, and 27 percent of women reported having quit their job to perform these caregiving tasks, compared with just 10 percent of men).[4] Another Pew survey shows that 41 percent of working mothers report that being a mother makes it harder to advance in their careers, compared with just 20 percent of working fathers who said the same.[5]

Women are also continuing to experience cultural stereotypes at work. Heilman and Chen find that in psychological experiments, women are viewed 14 percent less positively than men if they volunteer to stay late and work on a project and 12 percent more negatively than men if they do not.[6] Moreover, Williams and Dempsey note that even women in high-earning professions such as law and medicine continue to be consigned to the "office housework" that includes planning parties, ordering food, and doing other undervalued, administrative tasks.[7] These studies reveal that there is essentially a *gap* between the changes in public policy over the last twenty-five years or so and the degree to which women feel the impact of these policies in their own lives.

Scholars have long studied the gap between the law on the books and the law in action—or, as Kitty Calavita refers to it, "the talk vs. the walk of law."[8] One way of trying to understand this gap is to examine how people come to experience and interpret law on the ground—something known as "legal consciousness." Exploring the way in which women come to know, interpret, and use these laws and policies in their daily lives can yield important insights into the efficacy of the laws and policies themselves. In order to better understand why work/life balance laws and policies have not lived up to their promise to create significant social change, it is necessary to explore them in action, in the lives of the very women they are meant to affect. If these laws and policies are not easing the tensions between work and family life in a meaningful way for women, then how are women experiencing them?

This book disentangles the factors affecting how individual women come to understand work/life balance laws and policies and how that understanding is then reflected in the decision-making processes of these women around their rights. Recognizing how legal consciousness is formed around a given policy can help to clarify whether a policy is truly effective in achieving its stated goals. In order to do this, I conducted forty-eight in-depth interviews with women in two workplace settings: public universities and the U.S. military. Comparing interview data across these two sites, I explore three dimensions that matter to the construction of legal consciousness: the instrumental, the institutional, and the ideological.

Public universities and the U.S. military are particularly good sites to investigate the significance of institutional culture on the formation of legal consciousness. Both public universities and the U.S. military have unique and easily identifiable workplace cultures. These cultures can also be said to generally transfer from base to base, or from university to university, as part of larger professions. Both are also highly reliant on hierarchical structures and explicitly engaged in forms of public service. For these reasons and others that I explore in the book, these work-place settings lend themselves well to analytical comparison.

This book is ultimately an exploration of the ways in which the individual and the social are connected in the formation and significance of legal consciousness. The institutional comparison provided in this study, coupled with attention to the factors that have an impact on legal consciousness formation, allows me to illuminate this connection. Legal consciousness around work/life balance policies is formed through formal and informal institutional norms and structures, the communication of ideology (in particular, the ideological construct of the "ideal worker"), and individual agency. This book shows that current policies aimed at achieving work/life balance are often proving to be problematic for women's career advancement, retention, and equality in the workplace.

Rights Consciousness and Rights Claiming

For years, law and society scholars have documented the interactions that individuals have with the law in their everyday lives.[9] They have also been interested in how individuals think about the law and in tracking the mutually constitutive relationship between legal action and legal consciousness.[10] Fundamentally, scholars who study the connection between *legal consciousness* and *legal mobilization* are interested in questions of how people use legal concepts, legal terminology, and other kinds of connections with the law in their everyday lives and when and how that matters for rights claiming. Ewick and Silbey offer perhaps the best description of legal consciousness and its impact on how people use the law, when they outline the concept of "legality."[11] Legality, they claim, is a socially constructed reality of daily life—a legal environment, within which individuals must navigate both formal and informal norms, ideas and practices. Legal consciousness then, for Ewick and Silbey, both shapes and is shaped by this legal environment. It can essentially be defined as "participation in the process of constructing legality."[12]

It seems reasonable that individuals may use rights language to make sense of their experiences and try to take some control over how they view themselves under the law. It is easy to see the connection between how individuals make sense of the law and their decision-making processes about whether to lay claim to rights within their given legal environment. Yet an important question concerning identity and individuals' relationship to the law remains: How do individuals come to use the language of the law to interpret their situations? Law and society scholars emphasize the mutually constitutive relationship between individuals and their society in developing and perpetuating the meanings of legal concepts such as "rights," and therefore the reciprocal nature of individual and collective legal consciousness.[13] As Elizabeth Schneider observes, rights claims shape public discourse, which in turn shapes political action and eventually the law.[14] It is not a direct relationship, she argues, but rather a dialectical one. The assertion of rights can limit a group's (or an individual's) possibilities, but can also help to move them forward—particularly in the context of the dialogue and introspection of the movement itself.[15]

It is this understanding of legal consciousness that I employ in this book. Legal consciousness is developed through intersubjective processes between society and individuals. Individuals' legal consciousness shapes how individuals think about law, both consciously and on a deeper, more instinctive level; it also shapes the decision-making processes that individuals undertake around choosing to mobilize law (or not) when they find themselves to be rights holders. Legal consciousness clearly involves both an awareness of one's legal environment, as well as participation in on ongoing discursive process of shaping that legal environment. In this book, I tease out the various factors that help to shape legal consciousness—particularly for individuals—within their legal environment. How specifically, is legal consciousness constructed around work/life balance policies? What factors might influence the way legal consciousness is formed among working mothers or mothers-to-be? Furthermore, how might legal consciousness help to explain the gap between the intention and presence of work/life balance policies and the experiences of women with these policies?

The answer to these questions lies in the connection between the individual and the social in legal consciousness construction.

As Susan Silbey argues, the best way for law and society scholars to move legal consciousness research forward is to go back to looking at how legal consciousness can be shaped by (and implicated in) hegemony.[16] Legal consciousness is not simply affected by hegemony; it also plays a key role in shaping and producing "the very same structures that are also experienced as external and constraining."[17] The recent institutional turn in political science and other disciplines is particularly useful for exploring this connection between legal consciousness and the production of hegemony. Institutions are social sites, where individuals interact with common rules, norms, and goals. By comparing individual legal consciousness and legal mobilization in distinct institutional settings, this book brings into focus the connection between the individual and the social in the production of legal consciousness and legal environments.

The conceptual framework of this book explores the factors with an impact on legal consciousness formation. This framework, initially proposed by Haltom and McCann, is particularly useful for tracing the connections between the social and the individual in the formation of legal consciousness.[18] This framework, which explores the instrumental, institutional, and ideological factors that contribute to the formation of legal consciousness, allows me in this analysis to conceptually disentangle the threads that comprise the sources of individual legal consciousness formation while simultaneously keeping an eye on the ways in which these threads of legal consciousness are hegemonic.

Institutional Context

The first dimension of analysis in this book focuses on the impact that institutional context has on shaping individuals' legal consciousness and decisions about rights claiming. This relationship between the individual and her institutional context is complex. Nevertheless, institutions are a particularly fruitful area for sociolegal inquiry into the significance of cultural context in the formation of legal consciousness. Institutions are more than the physical structure of a university or military base. They are also places that provide rules, norms, constraints, and structures to those who operate within them. Those who are part of an institution are also in a perpetual discourse with the institution; they are themselves helping to shape the institution's rules and norms. Institutions are the places within which it is easiest to see the social and the individual in conversation. Institutions both reflect larger social contexts (structures, ideas, rules and norms) and develop their own individual and unique contexts. These contexts are reflected and shaped by the individuals operating within institutional settings.

Institutional *context* is an important factor in shaping how individuals form their legal consciousness. As so many studies of rights mobilization have attested, legal consciousness is a significant factor in individuals' ability to rights-claim, or mobilize to implement rights. Individuals frequently must consider themselves as rights holders in order to rights-claim. An awareness of the law, however, while an important first step, does not in itself determine rights claiming. Context also plays an important role in determining whether individuals choose to rights-claim. John Gilliom's study of Appalachian welfare poor, for instance, demonstrates that the mere awareness of rights is not enough to cause individuals to mobilize to change unjust conditions.[19] The women in Gilliom's study are confronted not only with a lack of resources but a culture that creates "significant pressures and tendencies against rights-claiming in the everyday lives of these welfare mothers."[20] In this case, these women's' legal consciousness is clearly more than an awareness of rights. Rather, their legal consciousness—their understanding of rights and the context within which they must make decisions about claiming them—causes them to understand the futility of rights claiming within their given context.

Therefore, a simple formula does not exist whereby the presence of legal awareness leads to rights claiming. The context, both cultural and institutional, matters in that norms, rules, and practices present before (or after) the introduction of rights can constrain the ability of individuals to gain legal awareness and to rights-claim. These cultural and institutional norms play a critical role in constructing individual legal consciousness, with a significant impact on the decision-making processes around rights.

It is not simply the formal rules or structures of an institution that matter in shaping and constraining individual thought and behavior. Rather, *informal* rules, structures, and norms also develop and can be equally salient for individual legal consciousness and legal mobilization. Anna-Maria Marshall, for instance, notes that in the case of sexual harassment policies, "When women . . . fear retaliation for exercising their rights, then the remedial policies and procedures may be inadequate to address the underlying problems."[21] In her study, "women anticipate skeptical treatment by their supervisors" and modify their thinking and formal rights claiming in relation to this informal expectation.[22]

Both the formal and informal mechanisms by which individuals may be constrained or influenced within institutional settings must be taken into account when analyzing the ways in which women themselves often participate in constructing these institutional settings. Chapters 1 and 2, which offer an in-depth look at each case study, parse out the formal and informal rules, norms, and structures that the interview respondents identify as salient in the governing of their respective institutions.

Several scholars have already identified the workplace as a type of institution that is particularly prone to developing and perpetuating hegemonic norms and ideas.[23] Studies that take an institutionalist approach to the workplace are necessarily complicated by the diverse nature of workplaces. Indeed, some types of work can hardly be thought of as having an institutional structure in the traditional sense (e.g., those who operate small businesses online). Yet it is possible to argue that most employed Americans work within a defined institutional context—a doctor's office, a police station, a school, a corporation, a law firm, and so on.

The workplace is where many individuals acquire knowledge of their rights under various laws and public policies (e.g., in areas such as sexual harassment, discrimination, and worker's compensation) and where they choose to take up those rights—or not. Indeed, navigating rights within the workplace is not always a simple matter of finding out what you are entitled to and claiming it. Several studies have examined the complexities of implementing sexual harassment policy in the workplace, highlighting that a policy's existence alone is often not enough to encourage rights claiming. These studies reveal the significance of institutional context, including norms, attitudes, relationships, and workplace-specific rules that constrain individual decision making.[24]

Other studies of employees in their workplace settings have focused on the important role of ideology, its cultivation in the workplace, and how it is absorbed or resisted by workers.[25] Specifically in the area of maternity and family leave policies, some scholars document the effects of institutional contexts on individual decision making and ideology formation. Mason et al., for instance, examine the norms and expectations within university settings and their effects on individual decision making that have resulted in more female than male faculty members "leaking" from the academic pipeline.[26] Joan Williams has also documented the existence of an "ideal worker" concept within workplace contexts and has argued that it has detrimental effects on women's decisions to seek out or take up maternity leave rights.[27]

The multiple layers of law and policy at work in the area of work/life balance policy, including both formal and informal rules and norms, should be of particular interest to sociolegal scholars. Yet to date, few sociolegal scholars have explored work/life balance laws and policies and the significance of their institutional contexts. Catherine Albiston, whose book looks closely at the FMLA in action in the workplace, is one notable exception.[28] She places a significant emphasis on institutional context in shaping individual rights consciousness and, in particular, constraining the ability of individuals to rights-claim.

Other research on legal consciousness formation in the workplace has not yet looked comparatively at institutional contexts such as the one offered here of public universities and the U.S. military. This institutional comparison helps to expand some of Albiston's key observations about institutional context. In particular, this comparison allows for the analytical sharpening of the significance of power relations within institutions. In this book,

I demonstrate that formal institutional structures such as rank are interpreted and navigated using a host of informal norms. I conclude that these formal and informal norms, which manifest themselves similarly (though distinctly in both case studies), are indeed significant in contributing to women's legal consciousness formation and are often constraining on these women's ability to rights-claim. Yet I also find evidence that women can and do use these same formal and informal norms to challenge hegemony within their institutional settings.

The Role of Ideology

The second dimension of analysis in this book concentrates on the significance of ideology in legal consciousness formation. *Ideology* is a term with multiple meanings within scholarly literatures. Indeed, even more narrowly within sociolegal scholarship, this term has taken on a diverse array of meanings. Its broad interpretation, however, has yet to divest ideology of its analytical and explanatory usefulness. As we will see, there is an immense significance to the ideological construct of the ideal worker for the production of legal consciousness around work/life balance law and policy.

For Patricia Ewick, ideology is a *"process* of meaning making that serves power."[29] That ideology is a process implies that it is continually being constructed. Ideology is meaning making that is taking place on both the social level of public discourse and the individual level, in a perpetual cycle. In a way, ideology can be understood as the missing link between social and individual legal consciousness. As individuals try to make sense of the world around them, they draw on social ideological frameworks and in turn contribute to them.

Stuart Scheingold takes this one step further, indicating that ideology is not simply a cognitive process, but something that is used for political ends, in that it "elicits support, mobilizes energies, and coordinates the activities of its adherents."[30] For Scheingold, ideology provides a framework around which individuals can collect, organize, and take political action. It is inherently *social*. Moreover, in Scheingold's understanding of ideology, these powerful symbolic frameworks (like his "myth of rights") can be employed in the service of power or in resistance to it.

Ideology can ultimately be understood as a lens. It is a way for individuals to view the world and make sense of what they are seeing. This lens then gives them a way to connect to one another by seeing the world in a similar way. Furthermore, most individuals do not simply possess a single ideology. Indeed, they often harbor multiple, even conflicting, ideologies. Yet they are able to make connections with others with overlapping ideological frameworks and organize around a common meaning. Ideology is inherently useful for understanding the formation of legal consciousness, specifically because it is something that individuals use to connect to the social—in the service of hegemony or in resistance to it.

In their study of tort reform, Haltom and McCann consider ideology to be at work alongside and within both instrumental design and institutional practices, and thus their discussion of ideology is interwoven with their analysis of the other two dimensions: instrumental actors and institutions.[31] "In this sense," they write, "ideology refers to intersubjective conventions that constitute social life less by dictating or impeding thought than by inviting, encouraging, privileging, and facilitating certain types of interpretive constructions over others."[32] The ideology that Haltom and McCann are focused on is the popular cultural norm of "individual responsibility" and "populist antipathy toward formal state intervention in socioeconomic life."[33] The authors are particularly interested in observing how this ideology is then brought into discussions of tort reform in order to imbue arguments with "moral power" and thus have an impact on legal consciousness.

Just as Haltom and McCann focus on a particular ideological strain, this book focuses on a particular ideology that has developed since the advent of the industrial revolution and took hold of the American imagination particularly in the mid-twentieth century—what Joan Williams refers to as the ideology of domesticity.[34] I later discuss in more detail how this ideology has developed over time and is the source of an ideological construct of the ideal worker that is pervasive within American workplaces.

Instrumental Design, Strategic Action

The third and final dimension of this book's analysis focuses on the significance of instrumental design in the formation of legal consciousness. The instrumental factor of this approach might be viewed as the individual unit of analysis. For Haltom and McCann, who were interested in analyzing the production of legal knowledge on a broader social level, it was important to pay the closest attention to instrumental actors who are elites, such as groups or individuals who see themselves as "tort reformers" and are thus trying to sway public discourse along lines that serve their political and ideological agendas.[35] I am most interested in analyzing the interwoven relationship among institutions, ideology, and instrumental actors in order to explain the individual and her connection to the social in forming her rights consciousness. Therefore, it is important to consider instrumental designs as the actions of individuals who are working with agency to affect their own or others' legal consciousness.

As Haltom and McCann point out, "one especially significant aspect of most instrumental contests is the effort of some parties to control, or to influence, what others do or do not know and count or discount as relevant knowledge."[36] Instrumental design, in the context of this analysis, might look less like politicians or activists interested in pushing tort reform and more like a supervisor who is interested in getting the most out of an employee. The actions of that supervisor may be driven by a particular ideology and may have significant consequences for the legal knowledge that an employee is subject to and what "choices" she feels constrained by. In her study of employees claiming FMLA, for instance, Albiston finds that employees often tried to couch their rights claims in ways that would conform to managerial norms or expectations. As Albiston finds, employers did not actually ignore the law: "They complied at least partially by telling workers about their rights, or by allowing some workers to take leave. Nevertheless, they implemented the law in a way that emphasized managerial norms about work and schedules," such as rewarding production targets that undermined leave rights."[37]

Haltom and McCann also discuss the strategic nature of instrumental action.[38] For their analysis, this strategic action took the form of interest groups or elites using or proliferating certain types of knowledge and concealing others. However, this strategic element can again be employed in a more bottom-up analysis of legal consciousness. Individuals may, for instance, have strategic reasons for seeking out, proliferating, or concealing certain types of legal knowledge for the purposes of their own professional interests in a workplace environment. A female employee who wants to have a child, for instance, may seek out other women who have already claimed their rights in order to gain legal knowledge about the formal process of applying for a policy or for information about informal norms that may make claiming her rights difficult. This act would be strategic, in that it would have implications for her professionally but would also be a means of helping to shape the formation of her legal consciousness.

Institutional context, ideology, and instrumental design, argue Haltom and McCann, act together to construct legal consciousness. In some ways, it is almost nonsensical to try to separate their functions and consequences, since each necessarily relies on the other and all are working together in a consistent and often cyclical process. Nonetheless, separating them for the purpose of analysis, while maintaining an appreciation for their interconnectedness, allows scholars to glimpse with greater conceptual clarity what is important to the formation of legal consciousness.

Women and Work—Who Cares?

Working mothers present a paradox within an American cultural identity that values both the privacy of the home environment and the notion of equality in the public sphere. The rights available to them vary not only according to coverage under

FMLA but also from state to state and workplace to workplace. Some working women in America are entitled to no leave or work/life entitlements at all and must try to negotiate family care needs and financial needs within the means available to them only in the private sphere. Others have various levels of paid and unpaid leave promises under state or federal law or institution-specific policies on which they can draw to supplement their private negotiations between care needs and financial needs. This variability in terms of family leave offerings across the United States, from institution to institution (with variability sometimes within the institution as well), is why this book looks at all policies aimed at improving work/life balance rather than simply maternity leave. Additionally, in some workplaces, such as the U.S. military (as I discuss in Chapter 2), taking maternity leave is a very different experience from trying to gain access to other rights, such as breast-feeding accommodation. Including all work/life balance policies in this analysis offers a greater breadth of understanding how women must navigate the often complex terrain of their working environments in order to try to grasp the underlying promise of all of these policies: better work/life balance.

The relationship between the individual and the social in the context of women and the workplace has historically often been conceptualized as a dichotomy between the "public" and the "private" spheres. Feminist scholars producing work on women's equality in the workplace have most often understood the concept of a public/private dichotomy between family life and the nondomestic sphere as problematic for achieving gender equality.[39] The problem, according to these scholars, is that much of the movement to achieve equality for women has tried to address inequality in the public sphere (e.g., fighting for the vote, for entrance in the workforce) while inequality in the home has remained unrecognized and untreated. Yet as Okin points out, "the personal is political."[40] The private cannot be ignored, these scholars have argued, because it also profoundly affects the public. Therefore, the focus on work/life balance policies in this book is particularly appropriate, in that this is an area of the law where society is ostensibly interested in helping individuals to bridge the gap between their public and private selves.

In a society in which political campaigns are often waged on the issue of "family values," many women have fallen through the cracks of public policy; for them, the notion of public equality is a political fiction. In making a conscious decision to focus primarily on mothers and the family leave and other work/life law and policies that apply specifically to them, I acknowledge that I am rendering invisible the similar needs and struggles that many working fathers face.[41] However, this choice to narrow my study to women is rooted in my understanding of feminist legal theory, which highlights the unique challenges that women face due to the engendering of their bodies as "different" and thus inherently unequal to men's. Pregnancy is particularly a time when the difference of women's bodies is made public and they are thus exposed even further to "othering."[42] Additionally, feminist scholars recognize that social structures and institutions, which include the workplace, are inherently gendered, posing a unique challenge to women. Joan Williams points out that the status quo of the workplace is a gendered one, which means that women must navigate workplace norms that are inherently discriminatory toward them.[43] As Patricia Smith argues, the problem of structural inequality in the workplace is one of the key battles of feminism in the twenty-first century:

Traditional social structures essentially require women (but not men) to choose between a career and a family (or to balance one against the other, thus impairing both). . . . Men never had to make such a choice. . . . The more this tradition breaks down, however, the more the conflict between work and family responsibilities will become a problem for men as well as women. Thus, the question of how to restructure our institutions to resolve this conflict is one of the most pressing issues faced in the twenty-first century.[44]

While public discourse around work and family is on the rise, data on women in certain kinds of workplace settings are still scarce. Both public universities and the U.S. military are understudied kinds of workplaces. A few recent studies have yielded some important quantitative data on women and work/life balance policies in the academy.[45] Qualitative data on women's experiences as mothers in academia, however, have tended to find their way into memoirs and self-help books rather than scholarly analyses.[46] While there is a dearth of data on mothers in academia, data on women as mothers in the U.S. military are even scarcer. The most notable work on women and the U.S. military has focused on questions of gender and integration,[47] not women as mothers and workers. Additionally, the vast majority of this research has been in articles rather than books. Oral histories of U.S. women veterans of the wars in Iraq and Afghanistan exist in small numbers as part of oral history projects at universities such as the University of North Texas and the University of North Carolina, Greensboro. These oral histories, while occasionally touching on the subject of motherhood, do not focus on these questions. The interviews conducted for the study in this book therefore provide a valuable contribution to data on women as mothers and workers in the traditionally male-dominated institutions of public universities and the U.S. military.

The focus of this book is on the connection between the social and the individual in the formation of legal consciousness. Yet the fact remains that there are women who must negotiate the tension between the public and the private every day. This research has some important implications for employers and public policymakers. If social and environmental context are having as much or more of an effect on women's tendency to rights-claim as the policies themselves, then public and workplace policies will need to be reassessed in order to take these factors into account.

Methodology and Case Selection

Numerous scholars who look at rights claiming in the workplace have already highlighted the significance of institutional context in influencing rights consciousness and rights claiming.[48] Yet these studies do not undertake a comparative analysis of institutional contexts. This book engages in a comparison of workplace contexts. This comparison allows me to ascertain with greater clarity which aspects of legal consciousness are formed due to specific institutional factors and which are perhaps influenced through broader societal factors. A comparison of individual narratives from vastly differing sectors such as academia and the military offers much deeper insights into the importance of institutional structures in shaping legal consciousness, because one could expect to see much greater variation in institutional impact.

I chose to interview women faculty of all ranks from a small, public academic institution and a larger public institution, as well as women who are actively serving or have served in all branches of the U.S. military, including active duty, veterans, and reserves. The variation between the policies and practices of these research sites affords me the opportunity to compare different institutional environments, and women's interactions with them. In addition, by including women from this range of institutional settings I am able to document the narratives of participants with a wider range of ages and socioeconomic, racial and educational backgrounds.

This book draws on data from forty-eight in-depth interviews that I collected over a one-year period from 2012 to 2013. Twenty-four of these interviews were conducted with academic faculty and twenty-four with former and active-duty service members from various branches of the U.S. military (Army, Navy, Air Force and Air Force reserves, Marines, and Coast Guard). The ages of the women interviewed range from twenty-three to fifty-eight. Some of the women who participated do not have children but are thinking about becoming pregnant or adopting in the near future. Other participants have one or more children. The levels of career achievement (and consequently income levels) vary widely among the women interviewed. Among military women, fifteen of the women are enlisted members in ranks ranging from E-3 to E-7,[49] and nine of the women are or were officers, with the highest rank represented being a current colonel in the Air Force. Among faculty women, I spoke with fifteen women at a small public university in the South and nine women at a large, multicampus university in the Northeast. Thirteen women are assistant professors on the tenure track, five women are tenured associate professors, and six are adjuncts, instructors, or visiting assistant professors. Among all of the participants, race, ethnicity, and sexuality do not vary considerably. Only three participants identified themselves as nonwhite, and only one participant identified herself as being in a same-sex relationship. Most of the participants are married or living with a partner, with only six identifying as single or separated. Finally, 90 percent of the women interviewed also identified themselves as either the primary breadwinner or "equal" in regard to wage earning in their households.[50] (See Tables 1 and 2 in the appendix for a list of the respondents.)

Interview subjects at the public universities were recruited using e-mails to general faculty listservs and by word of mouth. Interview subjects for the U.S. military case study were recruited using posts on various relevant online discussion boards and websites (e.g., the Facebook page for Breastfeeding in Combat Boots) and word-of-mouth. Each woman interviewed was asked the same series of loosely organized questions about her experiences with taking maternity leave at her place of work, which included questions about her experiences with planning to have children, pregnancy or adoption, taking leave, finding information about policies, returning to work, and interactions with colleagues or supervisors regarding work/family issues. Each interviewee was also asked a series of questions about her opinions regarding maternity leave in the United States and at her place of work and about how she might like to change policies, if at all. All of these questions were covered in each interview; however, the format and structure of each interview was unique, and certain follow-up questions differed based on each individual's related experiences.

In analyzing the interview data, I used interpretive methods to explore women's use of legal or rights-based language and their formation of concepts and justifications for their actions in relation to the policies to which they are entitled concerning work/life balance. The choice of interpretive methods over something like content analysis here is appropriate, in that I was interested in a bottom-up development of concepts rather than mapping preexisting terms and models onto these women's language and consciousness. Since I am interested in how their legal consciousness is formed, it was appropriate to use a method that would allow inductive techniques for determining how women's knowledge of and interaction with the law had been influenced.[51] I conducted each interview myself, making note of major themes addressed at the time. I then reread each interview multiple times, noting major themes that emerged consistently throughout each case study. Finally, once I had identified several of the major themes I wanted to address in the analysis, I systematically coded each transcript for these themes.

Outline of the Book

Chapters 1 and 2 provide separate and detailed analyses of the interview data, which outline the experiences of women trying to navigate their rights within their respective workplaces. These chapters explore both the formal and informal rules that women in each institution must navigate in order to understand and make decisions about their rights to work/life balance within their particular institutional setting.

Chapters 3, 4, and 5 are organized around the three threads of the theoretical framework: the instrumental, the institutional, and the ideological. These chapters compare the case studies and allow detailed examination of each thread of the framework. The Conclusion provides a summary of the analysis, as well as a discussion of the implications of this research for public policy, and for scholarship on legal consciousness and social change.

1

Navigating the Rules in Public Universities

Constance is a thirty-nine-year-old assistant professor in her first year of a tenure-track position at a small public university in the American South. While on the academic job market in the year prior to our interview, Constance admits to having struggled with whether to get pregnant. "I'm probably in a little bit of an unusual situation because of my age. . . . We've had some difficulty—not getting pregnant, but I had some losses, so I knew I was going to have to start work pregnant." When I spoke with her, Constance had just given birth. She says she timed her pregnancy so that she would give birth during the summer months, thereby hoping to avoid any impact on her teaching. This timing was also important because "I knew, because I had calculated all of this out, that I would not have maternity leave or modified duties because I hadn't been employed here for a year. . . . I thought maybe they would kind of swing it, or maybe they would help me out with something, but I didn't know, and so that's why I had to—I timed it so I would have the baby in summer."

Constance says that she struggled considerably with the implications that starting a family would have on her career. She recounts feeling the dual pressure of trying to become a first-time parent at her age while at the same time starting a new job. Constance says she felt comfortable trying to get pregnant only in the window of time that would have allowed her to have her baby in the summer before she started her job, because "I was worried about how it would look at my job. . . . I mean, I am a good worker, right? I'm a responsible person, and I didn't want to start off on . . . what seemed like they would think of as an irresponsible thing."

Constance is simultaneously beginning her new role as a mother as well as her career as a tenure-track faculty member. The tension that she feels between her personal and professional life is one that other faculty members interviewed in this study expressed over and over again . Just like Constance, each of these women must consider her own circumstances when making decisions about her rights in pursuit of work/life balance. However, these faculty members, like Constance, must also consider both the formal and informal rules governing their institutions and how they will respond to those rules.

This chapter is the first of two in-depth looks at the case studies presented in this book. The goal of these chapters is to document the expression of legal consciousness among the interview participants in each institutional setting and highlight the most common themes and language the respondents employed. In these chapters, I explore women's personal narratives and present their own explanations as to what factors influenced their interpretation of and decision making around work/life balance laws and policies. These case study chapters paint a detailed picture of how women working in public universities and the U.S. military express their legal consciousness. Chapters 1 and 2 are also a springboard for exploring in more detail the formation of these women's legal consciousness, as women discuss how they have navigated the *formal* rules and structures and *informal* norms of their respective institutions.[1]

In this chapter and the next, I discuss some of the most common themes that emerged in the interviews, and they are organized in such a way so as to highlight how the respondents discussed interacting with work/life policies on both formal and informal levels. Each theme discussed begins with an illustration from one respondent's story. In this chapter, for instance, I present

Constance's story to introduce each major theme. I then support the presence of the theme with other women's stories. While each woman's experience is unique, the themes presented here are pervasive, reaching beyond one or a few of the women interviewed.

The Family and Medical Leave Act

Introduced in 1993, the Family and Medical Leave Act (FMLA) became the first, and still the only, federal policy regulating maternity leave in the United States.[2] The FMLA is a historical development in American policy that was not easily achieved. As early as 1984, drafts of the legislation began circulating through Congress, and it took a monumental and sustained lobbying effort to eventually achieve its passage under the Clinton administration.[3] The law affords employees twelve weeks of unpaid leave, but the law addresses more than maternity leave alone. The policy is also a federal attempt to take into account other issues that concern families trying to balance the tension between working and caring for a family. The FMLA applies to men as well and allows both sexes not only to take leave to be with a newborn child, but also affords unpaid leave for the purposes of adoption, caring for a sick child or an elderly relative, and for an employee's own medical emergency.

Despite its historic significance as a public policy achievement in the American political context, numerous studies have pointed out that the FMLA is a scant offering in the context of worldwide family leave policies.[4] According to a 2011 Human Rights Watch report, at least 178 countries have national laws that guarantee paid leave for new mothers, and more than 100 of those countries offer fourteen or more weeks of paid leave.[5] In contrast, 40 percent of American workers are ineligible to claim a right to leave under the FMLA. The twelve-week leave available under the FMLA is also unpaid, leading many who claim to "need" FMLA unable to take advantage of the policy. In one 2000 report, 77 percent of respondents who had reported that they needed leave also reported that they did not take the leave due to being unable to afford it.[6]

Although nearly 57 percent of women with children under the age of one year are in the workforce, the FMLA covers only approximately 58 percent of all employees in the United States. This is due to technicalities in the law, such as allowing businesses with fewer than fifty employees to opt out of the mandate to provide FMLA leave. Eighty-nine percent of American businesses are not covered under the FMLA.[7] Therefore, for many working mothers or mothers-to-be in the United States, federal law does not provide any leave protection. This is just one reason that many employers, including most colleges and universities, have introduced their own workplace-specific policies, aimed at improving work/life balance and providing incentives for the recruitment and retention of skilled women workers. Despite this more recent trend, only one-quarter of American workplaces offer any kind of paid maternity-related leave of any duration.[8]

Each of the women faculty members interviewed for this study who had worked at her institution for at least one year were eligible for FMLA benefits because the universities were large enough for the law to mandate its coverage.[9] However, some of the women in this study were also entitled to workplace-specific policies with additional benefits, such as some paid sick or family leave. I discuss the laws and policies that apply to the women in each case study in more detail later.

Women Faculty in Context

Academia provides an advantageous site in which to explore the impact of institutional context on the legal consciousness formation of individuals. While the academy has a long history of excluding women, in recent decades its commitment to the recruitment, retention, and promotion of women *seems* to have taken a turn for the better. Most academic institutions have implemented policies that would appear to be at the vanguard of the American workplace when it comes to accommodating the work/life balance needs of its employees. Work/life balance policies found within many academic institutions today include maternity and paternity leave, a stop-the-clock policy,[10] modification of academic duties, breast-feeding facilities and policies, and flexible work schedules. Such policies, in conjunction with the FMLA, make up the formal legal landscape within which faculty operate.

Despite these efforts within academia, recent studies on the effectiveness of policies such as maternity leave and stop-the-clock in achieving their goals of equality of opportunity have demonstrated a gap between intention and effect. Thornton's use of survey data from seventy-six colleges and universities indicates that many institutions are not correctly evaluating the research periods of faculty who have used stop-the-clock policies.[11] Similar discrepancies and even evidence of overt discrimination were also found in a 2004 American Association of University Women (AAUW) Educational Foundation survey.[12] Other research has produced compelling evidence that women with children in academia experience much greater challenges to success than their peers in other professions, such as law and medicine.[13] While roughly equal numbers of males and females may enter Ph.D. programs, women are "leaking" from the "academic pipeline," so that they are consistently underrepresented in the upper ranks of virtually all areas of higher education.[14]

Explaining these discrepancies appears to be a complex matter. Lynn O'Brien Hallstein and Andrea O'Reilly, among others, argue that academic women face a unique set of circumstances that produce these inequitable results. In the opening to their 2012 book on academic motherhood, they summarize several studies that compare academic women with those in other professional occupations. Moreover, female academics have the highest rate of childlessness[15] and are less likely to be partnered and more likely to be separated or divorced.[16] In addition, O'Brien Hallstein and O'Reilly note, postsecondary teachers receive considerably lower wages and face more competitive job markets relative to other professions such as lawyers and physicians.[17] Finally, some evidence points to large inequities in working hours, when both public and private labor are accounted for, between women and men, as being a possible explanation for the discrepancies between men and women in attaining the highest levels of professional achievement in academia.[18]

The biggest factor that appears to be affecting this position of academic women, according to much of the scholarship, is that the years required for professional training and development among academic women are much longer than those in other professions.[19] Wolfinger, Mason, and Goulden articulate this career trajectory's challenges to motherhood very well:

After four to eight years in graduate school, assistant professors have about six years to publish or perish. Only after tenure and promotion from assistant to associate professor are faculty members assured of job security. The median doctorate recipient is already 33 or 34 years of age; after a probationary assistant professorship, close to 40. In terms of career development this would be an ideal time for female professors to start their families, but biologically they are already past prime childbearing age.[20]

This body of research on the challenges facing women in academia who wish to parent contributes to, and reinforces, a "negative narrative," according to Kelly Ward and Lisa Wolf-Wendel. Empirical studies such as those discussed above have joined more anecdotal storytelling, such as that in books and blogs like *Mama, PhD*,[21] to create a "mystique" that "set[s] up an expectation that make[s] it difficult to imagine how a mother in today's society would be able to balance work and family, especially in a tenure-track position." Ward and Wolf-Wendel argue that while there is plenty of evidence to back this negative narrative, in fact women in the academy *can* balance work and family, and they (and others) dedicate books to discussing how to make these challenging professional circumstances more navigable for women.[22]

Books such as these focus not only on outlining suggestions for formal policy improvements at the institutional level but also provide academic women with advice on how better to navigate academic norms and cultures in order to mitigate certain challenges. In *Professor Mommy*, for instance, authors Rachel Connelly and Kristen Ghodsee advise women to be cautious in trusting or confiding in other academic women—particularly "senior women":

There was a time when the feminist movement encouraged us to think of all women as belonging to one big sisterhood. . . . The truth is that academia is a competitive business, and the people who have succeeded made lifestyle choices that supported their goals. This is especially true for women of a previous generation. . . . They were often forced to make a choice between family and career. . . . Given the sacrifices most of them had to make, they may be even more critical of you than some of your senior male colleagues.[23]

Women faculty are not unaware of this discourse in the literature. Even if they are not aware of what policies apply specifically to them before becoming pregnant or adopting, academic women are often very articulate about the norms and expectations of their profession regarding work and family balance. Academic women are aware that they must involve themselves in both formal and informal navigation of their workplace environments. By engaging them in conversations about their navigation of these formal and informal structures, it is possible to observe how academic women's ideas about work/life policies are shaped and how those ideas connect to their decision making regarding rights and rights claiming.

Navigating the Formal and the Informal in Academia

Navigating Formal Structures

The interview data are derived from conversations with women at two distinct universities. The first, where fifteen of the participants are employed, is a small, public institution located in the Southeast United States and employs roughly five hundred full-time faculty members. For ease of discussion, I assigned this institution the pseudonym Elm University. Elm University is located in a "right-to-work" state, so the faculty members do not belong to a union. All faculty (including visiting faculty and adjuncts) who have worked at Elm for at least one year, and at least 1,250 hours in the previous year, are entitled to twelve weeks of unpaid FMLA leave, during which time they may use any accumulated sick or vacation time to receive pay. In addition, all faculty (but excluding visiting faculty and adjuncts) who have worked at Elm for at least one year are entitled to take advantage of a modified-duties policy, which must be taken in the semester of birth or adoption or in the subsequent semester, and may be used equally by both women and men. Faculty are expected to continue to work full time, but duties may be modified so that, for example, teaching expectations may be replaced with administrative duties, with the goal of creating a more flexible working environment in the months immediately following childbirth or adoption. Requests for modified duties are formulated in an agreement between the employee and his or her department chair and then submitted to the university's provost for approval. Faculty members who are on the tenure track at Elm are also eligible to stop their tenure clocks for one year. But women who are breast-feeding at the institution are not covered formally under state law or institutional policy. All of the faculty participants in this study did have the right, under federal law, to receive "reasonable" break time and accommodations for breast-feeding due to an amendment of the Fair Labor Standards Act passed as part of the 2010 Patient Protection and Affordable Care Act. At the time that these interviews were conducted, these provisions were not yet widely known or implemented. Additionally, many of the women faculty interviewed recounted experiences with breast-feeding that took place prior to 2010.

The second institution ("Oak University"), where nine interview participants were recruited, differs significantly from the first in a number of ways. Institutionally, Oak is a much larger public university (employing twenty-five thousand faculty and instructional staff), located in the Northeast, and is composed of several distinct colleges. Perhaps most significant, faculty members at Oak, including visiting instructors, are unionized. Within the past five years, Oak's faculty union negotiated a paid parental leave agreement that applies to all faculty members (men and women, including visiting professors and adjuncts) who are employed at the university for at least one year and are paid for eight weeks. All faculty members are also eligible to take the twelve weeks unpaid FMLA if they have been employed for one year, working more than 1,250 hours that year. However, the eight weeks of paid leave may not be taken in addition to the twelve weeks of FMLA (in other words, employees are not entitled to twenty weeks of leave). Rather, they are entitled to eight weeks of paid leave and four weeks of additional unpaid leave. As at Elm, women or men on the tenure track at Oak University who have or adopt a child are also eligible to stop their tenure clock for one year. Finally, in the state where this institution is located, female employees who are breast-feeding are eligible for unpaid break time to express milk and may request a reasonable location in which to do so.

At both public universities in this study employees are eligible for multiple work/life policies, which may vary depending on their rank or status within the institution. This complexity can cause confusion not just for individual employees but also often for department chairs and even, occasionally, for human resources (HR) offices. When beginning her new tenure-track job, for instance, Constance tried to time her pregnancy so that she would give birth in the summer. This was not just to avoid, as she suggested, looking "irresponsible." Constance says that she also was fairly sure that she would not be entitled to a formal leave policy under FMLA or any university policies in her first year of work, but she was unclear as to whether her department chair might "kinda swing it, or maybe they would help me out with something." Indeed, when she approached her chair (who she describes as being "shocked" when she told him of her pregnancy), he was willing to help her put in a proposal for modified duties. However, the chair himself was confused as to whether she would qualify for the policy. The proposal was turned down by the provost's office, as Constance had suspected, because she had not yet been working there for a year. To make up for this, her chair gave Constance a course release for the fall semester— something that was within his discretion to grant.

Constance's confusion over what she was formally entitled to was largely due to her exceptional circumstances of having a baby in her first year of employment. Yet for some faculty, their confusion is due to a breakdown in the way that formal structures are supposed to operate. Nora, for instance, a forty-eight-year-old associate professor at Elm, says that an HR officer misinformed her that she was not entitled to FMLA because she was adopting rather than giving birth. It was not until over a year later, when adopting her second child, that Nora was compensated for this missed time. At Oak University, Paige, who is now forty-nine but was younger and an assistant tenure-track professor at the time of giving birth to her second child, says that her HR department also misinformed her as to her rights and responsibilities concerning FMLA. Taking the unpaid leave during the spring semester meant that she lost her health insurance benefits for that period, requiring her to pay for COBRA (the federal Consolidated Omnibus Budget Reconciliation Act).[24] But what Paige hadn't realized was that this meant she also lost her benefits for the summer that year as well. She complains, "So I wound up having to pay COBRA for June, July, and August, because I had taken the spring off, which I did—which nobody—I mean, nobody in HR told me that. I mean they gave me terrible advice, they really did."

While misinformation by HR departments was not typical among respondents, the complexity of coverage under the policies does appear to have caused women faculty difficulties along other points of formal claim processes. For instance, a lack of clarity from supervisors or department chairs about these policies and which employees they cover was more common. Courtney, a forty-three-year-old assistant professor on the tenure track at Oak who is thinking about having or adopting a child, says, "You know, part of the concern is also just not really understanding what the rules are." This confusion makes it more difficult for individual employees to know what their rights are, she says. She describes watching friends in other departments being "pressured" to make the timing of taking leave work in favor of their departments. "A friend of mine . . . was pressured not to teach during the spring semester because she was due three weeks in [to the semester] . . . or people who have been really pressured to come back early because the idea is, well, that's not really fair to your colleagues, you know, or certainly not fair to the college; you can't just come back in the middle of a term." Additionally,

Courtney points out, even when departments or department chairs may be more inclined to be supportive, often they lack experience themselves in implementing work/life policies. "I mean, not a single one of my female colleagues in my department has . . . dealt with a pregnancy during the ten years I've been here," she says, voicing her concern that her supervisor will not be able to clarify her rights for her if or when she does have a child.

Other women, though, believe their department chairs are one of the *best* sources of information about how to find out what they are entitled to and to assist with formal rights claims. For instance, Alex, a thirty-five-year-old associate professor at Elm who was still on the tenure track at the time of having her twins, says that her department chair was instrumental in helping her to submit and secure a successful modified-duties plan that she was extremely happy with. He helped to clarify her rights and ushered her through the process of claiming them at every step. "Procedurally . . . my department chair sent me the information, and it was like Greek to me, to be completely honest. So I just said, tell me what my chances are and what I need to know." In evaluating her experience, Alex says, "I think I really lucked out when—you know, they say 'you should pick your department chair as much as you should pick the job'—that was a good piece of advice for me. Because . . . I was still going to be married when I was interviewing, and so kids were off my radar at that point." Alex was not aware of a need to ask about her work/life entitlements at her institution and so did not ask these questions when applying for her job. Instead, she trusted that her department chair would help her with any rights claims she would need to make—which proved to be correct in her case. However, there are several potential disincentives to asking about work/life policies when applying for a job. As we will see later in this book, such inquiries might signal to a hiring committee that a candidate is not as "serious" about the job as other potential candidates. Such experiences with benefits inquiries are also complicated in an increasingly competitive job market, where often faculty do not have the luxury of having more than one job offer, regardless of their feelings about the benefits offered.

Vicky, an associate professor at Elm, is a department chair who says she explicitly tries to help junior faculty navigate their formal rights. She emphasizes the importance of supervisors being willing and able to educate employees about their rights:

If you're a second-year faculty member thinking about having a baby, you're not going to go to anybody and go, "I'm thinking about this, what should I do?" . . . But unless you've got a chair who is regularly saying to you, "So, if and when you decide you want to have a child, let's talk, you know, these are the policies that we'll look at together." . . . I know not every faculty member does that and not every chair does that.

Constance says that her fellow female faculty members were the first source to whom she turned when trying to find out what her formal entitlements were in her new workplace. "They made it helpful—they kind of explained it to me," she says. Charlotte, a thirty-five-year-old assistant professor at Elm with a one-year-old, also says that one of the best things her department chair did for her was to point her to another source of information regarding her rights and how to claim them—other mothers in her department:

In my, like, fourth month during the pregnancy I told my department chair and started to ask questions about, you know, what the process was, what the procedures were. She recommended I speak to other people in the building who had recently gone through the modified duties plan. . . . So I gathered the proposals from two other women in the department that had already gone through it and started looking through theirs.

Charlotte was not alone in finding her colleagues to be a useful source of information about her entitlements under work/life policies in her place of work, as well as strategies and ideas about how to claim those rights. The number one source of information regarding policy entitlements cited by women faculty in this study was their work colleagues. Tracey, a thirty-eight-year-old assistant professor at Oak, who has taken leave with two children since beginning her tenure-track job, says that her colleagues in other departments frequently approach her to find out whether their department chairs are applying policies correctly. She recounts,

There's a lot of people getting ready to have children, so [I] run into people, you know, going on maternity leave and stuff and discussing how their chairs are handling it and our department I found very supportive, but I know I heard stories of other people who were like, "Is it okay if my chair does, you know, this horrible thing or that horrible thing?"

For most of the academic women interviewed in this study, the trickiest aspect of navigating their formal entitlements seems to be the variable nature of those entitlements—in terms of how different types of employees are entitled to different things and how identical entitlements may be applied differently across the university. This confusion and frustration regarding variability are particularly acute at the smaller institution, Elm. Here, the unpaid FMLA leave is applicable to all types of full-time faculty (adjuncts, visiting, tenured, and tenure track alike). However, the modified-duties policy applies only to those who are tenured or on the tenure track. As was the case with Constance, the modified-duties policy also does not apply to individuals on the tenure track who have been employed at the university for less than one year. These discrepancies were the cause for complaint among several of the faculty who were interviewed. Valerie, for instance, a thirty-one-year-old visiting assistant professor at Elm, expressed frustration that her superiors were uninterested in helping her when she tried to raise the issue of visiting assistant professors not being covered under the modified-duties policy.

Another frustration for tenure-track and tenured faculty who are entitled to the modification-of-duties policy is in the perceived variability in how it is implemented. Alex was able to come to an arrangement where she was not required to teach during the semester following her delivery. Carol, too, a thirty-nine-year-old associate professor with a young child, says that this was her experience:

It seemed like there were a couple of people who had kids around the time that I did who felt that they had gotten a good modification of duties. And the impression I've gotten is that in the semesters since then they are scaling back and scaling back how much—how much of a modification they are actually able to give people. It did not seem to be the case, at the time that my proposal went through, that there was an expectation that you do forty hours work a week. I mean, my proposal doesn't show me doing forty hours work a week, I wasn't pretending I was gonna do forty hours work a week. And it seems like that is what's expected now.

The forty-hours-per-week expectation was certainly what Constance seemed to expect when she was submitting her request for modified duties (which the provost's office eventually turned down anyway). Constance says, "It's not supposed to be reduced work. You're supposed to be doing the same amount of work; you're just supposed to be doing it at home. For this reason, she says, she is grateful that her course reduction worked out instead of the modified-duties plan.

Formal policy therefore is by no means straightforward for academic women to claim, should they choose to, and finding out information about their entitlements can also be a challenge at times. Even at the larger university, where the eight weeks of paid leave is more universal, there is still some confusion and concern surrounding the correct application of formal policy, as Charlotte's statement implies. As these women have discussed, often the best resources for finding out about their entitlements and making formal rights claims have been other individuals—whether authority figures such as chairs or other colleagues who themselves have gone through the process of claiming rights.

Law and society scholarship has demonstrated that legal literacy—even within specific contexts where individuals function on a daily basis—is often fairly low.[25] Yet what knowledge of formal law individuals do pick up is often transmitted through social interaction.[26] Catherine Albiston, for instance, describes employees who create social spaces—or "informal networks for pooling knowledge about the law."[27] Additionally, Payne-Pikus, Hagan, and Nelson discuss the significance of mentoring as a key way of transmitting knowledge within legal firms.[28] Similarly, for female faculty members at Oak and Elm universities, it appears that networks of colleagues and their department chairs are the most common source of legal knowledge about how to navigate formal structures within their workplaces.

Navigating Informal Structures

As if formal rights claiming were not complicated enough, law and society research and other scholarship on institutions stress the significance of *informal* norms and structures in constraining individuals' information, perceived choices, and, ultimately, their behaviors, such as rights claiming.[29] Like the formal structures that academic women have to navigate, which have multiple layers, including federal and state law, institutional policies, and departmental implementation, informal norms and structures are also multilayered and complex. For instance, an individual woman may have to navigate the expectations of a supervisor, as well as the pressures placed on that supervisor from the provost, along with the beliefs of colleagues who say that "this is the way things have always been done."

One of the most powerful informal norms that academic women cited in this study was the image of the ideal worker—and their constant need to address their own relationship to this ideal. Joan Williams discusses the image of the ideal worker as someone who works full time, does not take sick leave, and is willing to put in overtime at the drop of a hat.[30] Faculty members in academia must "publish or perish," and in many other ways they are expected to demonstrate devotion to their job.[31] Stopping the tenure clock or taking six weeks or more of maternity leave—these are ways in which mothers are exempted from the expectations of their jobs in academia to have children. For academic women, the ideal worker norm means that they feel as though allowing their private life to be visible in their public workplace will make it more difficult for them to be viewed seriously as workers.

Constance's story is an excellent illustration of the pervasiveness of the ideal worker norm in the legal consciousness of female faculty members—and thus in their decision making regarding their rights to work/life policies. Constance was afraid to become pregnant within a window of time that would mean having a baby outside the summer months: "I was worried about how it would look at my job. . . . I felt bad. I felt like they'd been willing to take a chance on me, and so I didn't want to show up and not be a full employee." In order to remain within this window for childbirth, Constance underwent hormone treatments and says that had she not become pregnant within the ideal time period, she would have waited an additional year before trying again to become pregnant, at the age of forty. "I probably would have taken the risk and waited knowing well I'll just jack myself up with hormones, I'll just do IVF [in vitro fertilization], I'll do whatever." When asked how this knowledge made her feel, Constance says, "It makes me really angry," but says she would not have done anything differently.

Every one of the faculty members interviewed in this study referenced the ideal worker norm in her institution, either implicitly or explicitly (though, in the majority of interviews, the reference was explicit), emphasizing its salience in women's thoughts and their decision making. For some women, this norm was more salient than for others when making decisions about whether to rights-claim. Vicky, for instance, a mother of two at Elm who is in her forties, says that she worked from home during her entire maternity leave with her second child:

I was one of those really awful people who knew that they could take the time away, but would sit on the computer and do the work. Because [my son] had been born . . . early, I hadn't finished some of those projects that I was supposed to finish, I felt really compelled to do them, and so a week after he was born I was probably getting back on the computer and trying to do the work.

Several of the women at both institutions also confirmed that the ideal worker image was a reality in academia to some extent. Kay, a thirty-two-year-old assistant professor at Elm who is interested in having children, says, "Yes, I feel like if you really want to be a superstar in your field—if you want to be the big name—all the major names in my field are women who don't have children." This informal norm therefore affects decision making for many women, including her own, says Kay. "Then there's like the next tier, and they do have children, and they have fantastic output, but they're not—they're not on the same caliber as the upper echelons. And I'm okay with it. But that's also why I chose . . . where I am."

Kay is not alone in expressing that she made career choices that were shaped around this image of the ideal worker and her desire to sidestep the informal expectations that an academic career carries. Many other interviewees made similar statements. Valerie, for instance, says that she does not have any role models in her field to whom she can look to for guidance. She says, "The people who have tenure track jobs who are also female—I know one of them has specifically told me the reason 'I didn't have kids was because I was in a tenure track job.'" Valerie also describes shaping her career decisions around this norm: "So, I decided that I don't want tenure—I don't want to be in a tenure-track position, partially because of this issue. Not just maternity leave, but just the fact that our biological interval and our tenure window over-lap so much, and there's basically no accommodation for that." Valerie also expresses concerns about being informally penalized should she choose to claim her right to something like stopping the tenure clock. "I think, here, basically you can delay your ten-ure review for however long, for like a year. But it's like they're being reviewed for an extra year and everybody's putting pressure on you like why are you getting extra time?" Women like Valerie and Kay are shaping their legal consciousness concerning their rights and how they might be applied using their knowledge of informal norms in academia in general and in their institutions in particular. More significant, however, these informal norms are also shaping the behavior of women faculty. Their decisions about whether to have children, pursue career paths, and rights-claim are based on their knowledge and perceptions of informal norms.

Unlike formal policies, informal norms are not visible on HR websites or accessible in faculty handbooks. Instead, wom-en's consciousness of informal norms is informed through equally informal means—often through personal relationships or obser-vations of others' behavior in their immediate context (usually departments). In order to determine a chair's expectations, sev-eral women described having watched how he or she treated a colleague who had or adopted a baby. Constance says that she turned to other mothers in her department before speaking with her chair about her pregnancy to try to gauge what his reaction would be. She says she was relieved when they told her, "Just tell him . . . you know, he's really great; don't worry about it."

Several other women spoke of trying to ascertain the departmental mood by watching their chair for signs of his or her feelings about claiming work/life policies. Margaret, for instance, is a thirty-eight-year-old mother of a young child who had been teaching as an adjunct at Elm for several years when she decided to get pregnant. She says, "We really weren't . . . apprehensive. I think because . . . I'd sorta seen how other adjuncts did it . . . and the feeling I have from the general atmosphere in the department is family friendly." Still, says Margaret, she felt that it was important to tell her chair about her pregnancy as early as possible. "I felt like I was being the best employee I could be to tell him as soon as possible, so he'd have plenty of time to plan." As an adjunct faculty member, Margaret knew that her chair had a lot of discretion over how easy or how hard it would be for her to take the FMLA leave that she is legally entitled to. Margaret wanted to take the leave in the fall semester, because her baby was due in the summer. Given that Margaret is a contingent faculty member who depends on the annual renewal of her teaching contract, her chair could have refused to renew her contract in the spring. He could also have taken away her office or in other ways made her return to work difficult in ways that the FMLA has no means of protecting Margaret against. Being able to navigate the informal norms and expectations within her department, therefore, was essential for Margaret's decision making; she needed to be confident in her department's informal norms in order to feel secure enough to claim her formal right to unpaid leave.

In addition to observing colleagues' and supervisors' behaviors, as Margaret did, many of the women faculty described actively seeking out other women who had claimed work/life policies before them (or were trying to do so at the same time). Just as many women had described reaching out to their colleagues as a source of information about what formal rights were available to them and how to claim them, many of those interviewed also described connecting with others as a source of information about the informal norms in their institutions, and even for ideas about how best to navigate those norms. The most striking example of this networking is at Elm University, where many of the faculty members have begun to voice their dissatisfaction with the perceived variability in the way that the modified-duties policy has been implemented. Constance, for instance, had reached out to other women faculty members who had completed modified-duty requests when attempting to complete her own. She says she requested these "so I could see, you're just supposed to write kind of one paragraph, and it was kind of knowing what . . . the right words were, and what to put on the form."

In fact, Constance was the beneficiary of a network of women at Elm who make it a practice to share their modified-duty requests—particularly those who were successful. In addition, as Nora, a forty-eight-year-old mother of two and an associate professor at Elm, recounts, women at the university who are entitled to the policy have begun to actively resist what they believe is unfair about the policy. They do this by discussing and passing on tips for ways to manipulate the application process to individuals' advantage. Nora observes:

So there's all this sort of backroom talk about how to do this, and what to say and what not to say, and how to—how to get around the policy implications that the provost's office might levy upon you. So there's all this sort of hush-hush talk—"you might want to talk to so and so, but don't tell her I said this, and when you put your modification of duties proposal together, make sure you say this, but don't say that."

Nora and others within her network of friends and colleagues are using informal structures themselves to combat informal structures, which are causing what they deem to be unfair variability in the way that the policy is being implemented across the university. Women are therefore actively engaging informal structures as though they have important consequences (and indeed, they do)—consequences that are just as significant as, or perhaps more so than, those of the formal work/life policies.

Conclusion

Women's experiences with navigating their rights to work/ life policies on formal and informal levels enable us to see how decision making and rights assertion are affected by both the policies themselves and the institutional and cultural environment, which often operate in ways that are very distinct from the letter of the law. This division also clarifies what may have already been evident to readers, as it is to the women interviewed: whereas it is easy to conceptually separate formal structures and informal norms, this division becomes much less possible when an individual is attempting to claim her rights in reality. Several themes emerged in common among most or all of the interview participants in this study.

First, in terms of institutional traits, many of the women discuss the significance of rank and position in relation to both their decision making and their successes in rights claiming. This salience of rank seems to translate across both universities, with a greater significance at Elm, where faculty are not unionized and visiting assistant professors are not entitled to the same policies as tenure-track or tenured professors, as they are at Oak University. Second, women seem to cite the variability of policies, norms, and their applications at their institutions as being problematic. In the case of Elm University, this dissatisfaction has resulted in under-the-table resistance. Third, the salience of the ideal worker norm appears to be very strong at both universities, suggesting that this image permeates the entire profession.[32] Relatedly, women seem to use the language of "choice" quite often to explain their decision making in relation to ideal worker expectations—while at the same time expressing their anxiety about fitting into these expectations. Finally, and perhaps most significant, it is clear that supervisors and colleagues play key roles in providing information, informal support, and assistance in the formal process of rights claiming. As many of the women expressed, the disposition of a chair, dean, or provost can make the difference between a good experience claiming work/life policies and a nightmare scenario. In addition, it appears that colleagues are an important source of information and support for many women.

In turning to the second case study in this book, it quickly becomes clear that many of these themes are echoed in a very different institutional setting: the U.S. military. Lynn O'Brien Hallstein and Andrea O'Reilly are not necessarily incorrect in deeming academia to be a unique challenge to women who are interested in balancing work and family life.[33] However, the distinctive comparison of two workplace institutions in this project offers important perspective on the ways in which women's legal consciousness about work/life balance policies may be connected across institutional settings.

2

Navigating the Rules in the U.S. Military

Chloe, thirty-seven, is a captain in the U.S. Air Force with seventeen years of active-duty service. Her "plan is to retire at twenty, so I have three years left and I'm a major select." Chloe is also a mother of three (twin teenagers, and a preschooler), and at the time of our interview, she was expecting her fourth child. She recounts experiencing difficulties returning to work with both of her previous pregnancies. "When I came back to work after I had the twins, the leadership was fine . . . but my peers—I was treated like, 'Oh you've been off, you've been on vacation the whole time; now it's your turn to do the work!'" Seven months after returning to work with her now-preschooler, Chloe was sent overseas for a six-week training exercise and recounts battling her leadership for access to accommodations to express and store breast milk.

Under Air Force regulations, Chloe was obligated to inform her commanding officer within two weeks of a positive pregnancy test, which she did for her latest pregnancy in the months prior to our conversation. Initially thinking that her latest posting would offer her a fresh start after the difficulties she had experienced in her previous pregnancy, Chloe soon discovered that she would be facing tension between her work and her family life in her new posting as well. When she told her commander she was pregnant, he accused her of "quitting." "He said, 'I've never had an officer quit on me.' And I'm like, 'quit'? What are you talking about? Hold up. No, I got pregnant.' And I was then taken out of the exercise—I couldn't participate. I didn't quit. So once I had the conversation with him, like, in his mind, I'd quit. He didn't view it as a medical thing or whatever."

With each of her pregnancies, Chloe has found reconciling her role as officer and mother to be an uphill battle. Similar to Constance and other women faculty members, Chloe and her fellow service women must also navigate their own personal circumstances while also considering the formal and informal rules of their respective institutions. In this chapter, I present data collected from conversations with active-duty, reserve, and veteran U.S. servicewomen, highlighting the participants' interaction with work/life policies on both formal and informal levels. Chloe's story serves to illustrate each major theme, while the experiences of other women demonstrate how each of these themes emerges again and again across the interviews.

Servicewomen in Context

In January 2013, the Pentagon announced that it would lift the ban on women in combat roles. This announcement renewed a public debate about the changing role of women in the U.S. military. Servicewomen's advocates, such as the National Women's Law Center, praised the announcement: "This is a historic day. . . . Now if the best person for the job is a woman, she will no longer be barred from that job simply because of her gender," and it cited statistics on the number of women who had been serving in combat roles in Iraq and Afghanistan in the past decade. Critics of the move, such as U.S. Congressman Allen West, a retired Army officer, argued that it would "destroy the last bastions of American warrior culture all for the advancement of a misguided vision of fairness and equality," and he cited studies that suggested military cohesiveness might suffer as a result.[1]

While this book is not about the appropriate role of women in the military, this debate, and the typicality of this discourse in public discussion, is a meaningful backdrop to the experiences that the women interviewed contend with daily. Historically, women have always played significant roles in the U.S. military. However, following the end of World War II, their role in the services began to expand exponentially—mostly in traditionally female areas such as nursing and administrative staff. Then in the 1970s, women were admitted to Reserve Officer Training Corps (ROTC) programs and military academies, and the Department of Defense reversed policies that had previously required that women be discharged on pregnancy or adoption of children, giving them the choice to discharge or remain on active duty. In the 1990s, the war in the Persian Gulf marked a significant turning point in the public discourse on women in the U.S. military. Service members who were also mothers were visibly deploying in large numbers for the first time, a fact that did not escape media comment or public debate.[2] Since the Gulf War, and particularly with the advent of the wars in Iraq and Afghanistan, women's presence in the military has continued to grow, so that now women make up roughly 15 percent of all active-duty service personnel and almost 20 percent of reserve personnel.[3]

Despite their increased presence, as Laurie Weinstein and Francine D'Amico observe, "Women's military roles and contributions are often *invisible*—until women make themselves visible by challenging gender boundaries," such as Private First Class (Pfc.) Jessica Lynch, or "by appearing to make a mistake or to fail," such as former Army reservist Pfc. Lynndie England or Army Specialist Alexis Hutchinson.[4] In each of these cases, the role of women in the military is redebated on the public stage for a time and then once again quietly retired. In everyday life, however, military servicewomen must constantly contend with the same tensions that are raised in these brief public moments. One female service member observed, "Every day there's something to prove just because you're a female, and that's the way it is."[5]

Jennifer Hickes Lundquist notes in her study of job satisfaction in the military, that it is men who tend to be the most satisfied with their military careers.[6] Just why mothers may find the military a difficult career path is something that Mady

Weschler Segal speculates about, suggesting that both family and the military are "greedy institutions" that are in increasing conflict, especially as the ranks of women and mothers in the military swell.[7] Indeed, several other studies have pointed to high tensions between work and family commitments for female service members and the effects of these tensions. Vinokur, Pierce, and Buck, for instance, document the negative effect of work/life conflicts on the mental health of women in the Air Force.[8] Other studies have pointed to the sometimes difficult task of obtaining adequate child care arrangements[9] or the stress that deployment causes to couples or children[10] as potential causes for a unique tension between work and family among military service women. Finally, Kelley et al. found that work/life tensions and a "higher commitment to the motherhood role" predicted dissatisfaction with military careers and a lower retention rate among mothers serving in the Navy.[11]

Yet it is the prevalence of masculine culture that persists in the literature as an explanation for why servicewomen in general, and mothers in particular, still find the military to be a uniquely challenging career path. The "American warrior culture," to which Congressman Allen alludes, is a decidedly masculine one.[12] As Nancy Taber observes, while military occupations and branches each have their own idiosyncrasies, "they are inextricably connected and held together by an overarching institutional expectation that members' commitment should be to the military alone. It is within a male body that this commitment is expected to be best enacted."[13]

Other studies have documented the harm that such a strongly gendered work environment can cause its female employees. Emerald Archer demonstrates that "constant confrontation" with gendered stereotypes "may negatively impact a servicewoman's career" by influencing the perception of both male and female marines about the abilities of female marines (particularly in leadership roles).[14] This stereotyping has implications for women service members' opportunities for camaraderie, mentorship, and advancement, says Archer. Terms such as *dyke*, *whore*, or *bitch* are ones that scholars have found to be common terms for both male and female service members to use in reference to female service members.[15] As Francine D'Amico and others observe, this gendered environment also causes problems for military women who try to counter or report sexual advances, being labeled as "troublemakers" within their work environments.[16]

Military servicewomen are acutely aware of their institutional context, and the public discourse that surrounds their unique circumstances. In expressing their understanding of the work/life policies available to them in their workplace and how they go about making decisions about whether to claim their rights to those policies, the highly gendered environment of their workplaces plays an important role in how they choose to talk about their experiences. Like female academic faculty, military servicewomen are aware that they must navigate their workplace environments in both formal and informal ways in order to effectively claim their rights. By engaging them in conversations about how they navigate these formal and informal structures, it is possible to observe how military servicewomen's ideas about work/life policies are shaped and the ways in which those ideas connect to their decision making regarding rights and rights claiming.

Navigating the Formal and the Informal in the U.S. Military

Navigating Formal Structures

On a formal policy level, the Department of Defense and the various branches of the military offer some of the most generous work/life policies in the United States. The Department of Defense offered its servicewomen paid maternity leave long before the federal Family and Medical Leave Act was even passed.[17] At the time of my interviews, all branches of the military offered at least six weeks[18] of paid leave for birth or adoption, whereas only 16 percent of all U.S. employers offer paid maternity leave.[19] Service members may also negotiate with their supervisors to use annual leave in conjunction with this to provide an extra week or two. Servicewomen are not, however, covered under the FMLA and so do not have the option to take the full twelve weeks of unpaid leave provided by that legislation. In addition to maternity leave considerations, in 2008 the Department of Defense also approved paternity leave of ten days for all branches, and all branches with the exception of the Army have specific breast-feeding policies in place, including deployment deferment for breast-feeding mothers of up to twelve months.[20]

All service branches also heavily regulate the physical challenges of pregnancy individually, though there is a great deal of similarity in these regulations across branches. All service branches, for instance, have regulations that permit pregnant service members to modify or decrease their uniform and duty requirements at the discretion of her supervisor. For example, a woman in the later months of pregnancy may often request to wear sneakers rather than combat boots for comfort or to work reduced hours. In addition, a physical "profile"[21] is altered for a pregnant service member, restricting her automatically from certain special or routine physical activities that the rest of her unit may be involved in. Because servicewomen receive their health care from military facilities, a positive pregnancy test is not a private matter. Positive pregnancy tests are recorded in a physical profile, which is automatically passed on to the servicewoman's supervisor, meaning that if she does not inform her supervisor herself within a week or two, that supervisor will be informed of the pregnancy anyway. Finally, pregnancy is considered a valid reason for separation from any branch of the services. In other words, during her pregnancy, a servicewoman is given the option to honorably discharge from the military before her contract ends.

In navigating the formal policies that she was entitled to when taking leave, Chloe says that she never had a problem obtaining her leave, and in fact she was granted the ability to take additional weeks of annual leave with all three of her pregnancies. Interestingly, unlike the female faculty members discussed in Chapter 1, many of whom struggled to receive their full maternity leave benefits or felt that they had been unfairly treated in terms of the modified-duties policies or unpaid leave that they had received, not one of the military servicewomen interviewed said that she had had difficulty obtaining her six weeks of standard paid convalescent leave. That is not to say that all of the servicewomen were entirely happy with their experiences (a fact that will become evident shortly), but in terms of applying for and receiving six weeks of paid maternity leave, which was unbroken by requirements to work,[22] no servicewoman related an experience where she was not readily granted this. Most of the servicewomen voluntarily referred to convalescent leave for childbirth as a "right" in their interviews. As Chloe herself says, "When I signed up, I was told I get thirty days of paid leave [for childbirth], so I've earned it, so that's my right."

In addition, Chloe and several other women praised other formal structures in place in the military designed to support parents in their ranks. Chloe says, for example, "I think that adding the paternity leave was very helpful." Eileen, a thirty-three-year-old staff sergeant in the Air Force, is one of many servicewomen who also said that the affordable, high-quality day care available on base was an excellent formal support to her after returning to work with her first child. "The day care that they have is subsidized and it was really close by where I work, so I could go over and breastfeed or visit or—you know, that was really good. So overall, it—it was a pretty good experience." A few of the women interviewed also cited mandatory parenting and prenatal classes that were geared specifically to servicewomen as being particularly helpful, and required early in pregnancy, so that information about physical requirements and the length of postpartum leave were explained clearly at that point. Liv, for instance, a twenty-six-year-old first sergeant in the Army with an eight-month-old baby, says that these classes are where she learned about what she was entitled to in terms of her leave: "At [fort name redacted] they have a postwide pregnancy PT [physical training] program, and you have to go to a class and sign up for that and they tell you there, you know, after you have your baby, you have six weeks postpartum leave."

Apart from their universal success with claiming convalescent leave, what is perhaps most striking about the interviews with these servicewomen is that they all, to some degree, are aware of and have consulted a formal source of legal knowledge concerning their workplace rights—their branch's regulations. At some point in every interview, each servicewoman made a reference to the "regs"—or regulations—for her branch of the armed forces. Each branch has its own set of regulations to govern the activities and administration of that branch, and it is these regulations that make up the formal structures within which these servicewomen must claim their rights in the workplace. These regulations define what those rights are and how service members are to claim them. Each service member not only has access to these regulations for the purposes of gaining legal knowledge, but also is *encouraged* by her command to locate, become familiar with, and use these regulations to govern her behavior. As Joyce, a fifty-eight-year-old colonel in the Air Force, with grown children, puts it, "The beauty of having regulations—all the information's there. . . . It's not left open to anybody's interpretation or anybody's idea about what it should be; it's all there in black and white; you just have to look it up."

It is significant that the military identifies and anticipates the work/life conflicts of its female service members, codifying certain supportive measures for them to help mitigate those conflicts. Women such as Joyce express feeling a degree of security in being able to look up those regulations and bring them to the attention of their command should they wish to claim their rights. Law and society literature also identifies the inherent value in formal rights. In the context of litigation, both Sally Engle Merry and Michael McCann argue that while litigation may come with sizable risks and costs for those who wish to take it up, the fact remains that rights are indeed a club that the rights holder can wield.[23] However unwieldy, these scholars acknowledge, rights are surely better than no weapon at all. Rights can also provide recognition of identity, personhood, or prior harm, which can be invaluable to individuals who have previously gone unprotected by the law. Elizabeth Schneider notes that "the articulation of women's rights provides a sense of self and distinction for individual women, while at the same time giving women an important sense of collective activity."[24] Patricia Williams also recognizes that while formal rights probably have a limited effect on social change, they nevertheless have a symbolic importance—especially for those who have never before been recognized under the law in rights language—and that symbolism has power in and of itself, which makes formal rights significant.[25]

Navigating Informal Structures

Formal rights mean little in the face of powerful informal opposition.[26] Chloe's story at the beginning of this chapter illustrates all too clearly the impact of informal structures in weakening formal rights. She identifies three distinct ways that informal norms and structures played a significant role in influencing her thoughts and actions surrounding her rights under work/life balance policies. First, Chloe identifies an image of women as "nonideal" workers in the military, against which women must constantly contend. Second, she points to the importance of rank in the military and, in particular, a host of informal accepted behaviors associated with this more formal structure. Finally, she talks about the importance of informal relationships in influencing her decision making around formal policy.

The first, and perhaps most pervasive, of the informal norms that Chloe identifies is the salience of a stereotype of female service members as nonideal. In particular, Chloe talked about a certain image of the female service member as someone who is trying to get out of her duty. As her story illustrates, the thinking and behavior of Chloe's commander when she announced her pregnancy was directed by the impression that Chloe had "quit." Furthermore, she said that he has pulled her out of her previous job and placed her into "another job, that's a made-up job." When asked why Chloe thinks her new job is "made up," she replies, "Um, because it doesn't exist. Nobody had the job before me, and nobody will have the job after me." At the time of the interview, with seventeen years of service and at the rank of captain, Chloe felt as though she has been sidelined purposely and perceives this action as pointedly punitive. Chloe's commander does not have the ability to directly fire her, and so, Chloe believes, he has done the next best thing.

"They can't really fire me per se, when I've got so many years in. You know, so they can shove me off in a corner and give me some job that's essentially a made-up job. But my paycheck still comes in, so in that respect . . . I don't really have a threat." This may sound like a fortunate situation for Chloe—an easy, pointless job in return for her captain's salary. But this is not how Chloe sees it. She is frustrated that she is being treated as though she was no longer capable of doing her job once she became pregnant: "He treated me like I quit when I got pregnant. . . . I'm a highly productive individual. I would like to be gainfully employed."

Conversations with other servicewomen make it clear that this image of female service members is pervasive throughout of their stories and affects each of them on some level. For some women, like Chloe, the existence of this image is only mildly damaging: her supervisor essentially moved her to a "made-up" job. For others, this stereotype of pregnant servicewomen, or those who had become mothers, affected their relationships or positions in more significant ways, and they find themselves targets of what they see as unfair or unreasonable treatment as a result. Zoe, a twenty-nine-year-old veteran who served in the Air Force for three and a half years, says that when she found out she was pregnant and would be a single mother, she had never intended to leave her career. "I knew that it was gonna be a stressful experience, but I also knew that I was gonna have my schooling paid for, and that I would rise up in the ranks, and that this was what I had wanted to do since I could remember, you know?" She says, though, that she decided to get out when a supervisor approached her after learning of her pregnancy and threatened her. This threat, said Zoe, had everything to do with his expectation that she was trying to get out of something when she got pregnant:

The new NCOIC [noncommissioned officer in charge] said to me, "Mark my words, when you get back [from maternity leave], as soon as your son is six months old, I'm deploying your ass." And I was like, what? Oh—what? And he was like, "Yeah. You said you wanted to go on TCN [third country national, a type of temporary overseas duty] and deployments and all this kind of shit when you got here. You're leaving when your son's six months old, so get your little family care plan together.'"

Six months postpartum is the earliest that women in the Air Force are required to be eligible to deploy again.[27] Zoe insists that she knew she would potentially have to deploy but that her supervisor had made her feel as though she would be specifically targeted because he perceived that she was trying to get out of it and that made her start to think about leaving. "You know, I knew that it was a possibility. . . . As soon as any—like my bucket comes up, or whatever, I want to go . . . but it would have been vastly different, because I knew the intention isn't to separate me from my child. You know, and that was his intention. And to cause me kind of like undo, you know, stress."

Gina, a thirty-six-year-old chief petty officer in the Coast Guard, says that when she announced her pregnancy, her lieutenant commander (not her immediate supervisor, but the rank above him) "said that I am of no use to him anymore. And basically it had been all-out war between him and I from that moment on." Gina says that this officer would go out of his way to ensure that she was assigned duties that would be difficult for her to do when her daughter was very young. Gina and her husband are both in the Coast Guard, and were stationed in Guam at the time. Gina says that as soon as she returned from her maternity leave, this officer insisted that she be sent out on a case, despite the fact that her husband was currently out at sea:

I mean it's not like you can just . . . go for a day and then come back. I mean it was . . . probably gonna be a week-long thing and my daughter was nine weeks at that point, and I was breastfeeding. . . . It was ridiculous. He made the ship that my husband was on come back and drop my husband off, so that he then could watch our daughter to send me out to that island for absolutely no reason at all.

Gina argues that the worst part was knowing that "there were other qualified people that could have done it. . . . I think he was just making a point."

These stories illustrate a clear gap between the military regulations that are intended to make work/life balance more manageable for servicewomen (the law on the books) and the women's experiences with fearing job loss, the loss of status, or the loss of their commander or colleagues' respect because of pregnancy (the law in action). This sense of feeling targeted at work because of their rights claiming is not unique to military servicewomen. These same gaps between law and implementation have been documented by scholars in many areas of the law, such as sexual harassment policies,[28] and FMLA claimants in a corporate environment.[29] What is clear from both the literature and the evidence in these interviews is that these experiences—whether they affect an individual personally or are heard second-hand—have the power to change decision making and rights claiming (as it clearly did for Zoe, who had the option to stay in the military but chose to leave). Knowledge of the potential for these informal norms and attitudes among commanding officers and colleagues therefore becomes an important part of a servicewoman's legal consciousness development in her workplace.

The second source of informal ordering that Chloe mentions as being significant to her is the Air Force's ranking system—a system that is formal in structure but with power that extends beyond its formal parameters. During her first pregnancy, with her twins, Chloe needed to reduce working hours and eventually go on bed rest. The decision to reduce hours and go on bed rest was not Chloe's; her physician wrote the prescription for her profile, and in the Air Force, what the profile says the service member is physically able to do is what the service member must do and no more. Chloe's first sergeant, however, questioned the decision. "I remember the first sergeant questioned why I even got put on half-days and then why I was getting preference. Like, questioned the medical necessity for me to have reduced hours. . . . I was basically so low ranking and young . . . I just said, "Okay, whatever"; you know, whatever they told me to do, that's what I did." The decision to alter her profile, however, ultimately lay with Chloe's physician, so nothing more was said about it.

Following her second pregnancy, Chloe found herself once again on the wrong side of her immediate supervisor's discretionary powers. When her daughter was seven months old, Chloe was told that she would be sent on a short-notice tasking overseas for six weeks. She was given ten days to prepare for this deployment, despite the fact that she was breast-feeding her daughter at the time. "In the Air Force regulation," Chloe says, "commanders can use their discretion and not deploy them or whatever. And mine chose to. . . . Now I never once asked to get out of it. I never went to anybody and said, 'Hey can you not send me,' cause I didn't really feel like that was an option I had." Chloe's commander at the time, a woman, would have been within her formal jurisdiction to allow Chloe to defer deployment for an additional few months until she had finished breast-feeding her daughter. She was also within her jurisdiction to *not* exercise this authority, and she made it clear to Chloe that she was not going to do so. Chloe would have been within her rights to request that her commander allow her to defer the deployment, and she also chose not to do so. She cites her low rank as one reason that she did not exercise her right to make that request.

Rank, and the power differentials associated with workplace hierarchy, are not exclusive to the military, but the military's very core mission means that adherence to ranking means that its salience is arguably greater in this working context than in others. Several scholars have documented the significance of unequal power structures in the workplace and its effects on rights mobilization and rights consciousness.[30] Many of the servicewomen interviewed for this study echoed Chloe in discussing the significance of the structure of military hierarchy and rank to their personal experience. While rank itself is a formal structure, much of its organizational power derives from informal norms. Subordination in rank requires deference to authority, and finding the line between when an individual should defer versus when she should challenge authority under formal regulations that are in her favor is a fine line—one that many servicewomen are reluctant to cross. Indeed, the chain of command is the first thing that service members are taught upon entry, and serious consequences result in breaking that chain of command.[31]

Piper, a twenty-three-year-old former Army specialist who, at the time of our conversation, had just finished her contract, has a young son and is intending to study to pursue another career path. Piper says that she requested using her annual leave after her six-week convalescent leave, but her chain of command refused. "And basically the way the military works is if you're pregnant and you want an extended period of time, as long as your chain of command okays it, you can have more time. My chain of command didn't want me to have any extra time. So I got six weeks, and then I had to go back to work," she says. When asked whether she felt she had a choice to take the two extra weeks, Piper says, "Um, if I would have pressed for it, I could have taken the extra two or three weeks, however long I wanted, but I didn't really press for it." She says that her supervisor had told her to save the time for doctor's appointments or other needed time off for her son. She says that she's fine with the outcome because "when I got out of the military I had a whole lot of days saved up, so I could end my job sooner, and still get paid for it." Whether or not Piper was happy with the outcome, the fact remains that her initial request was denied, and, though she could have pushed harder to use her additional leave when she wanted to, she chose not to.

Jane, a twenty-nine-year-old captain in the Marines, says that rank has everything to do with young enlisted service members not speaking up for themselves regarding their rights. She claims that a lot of the ease that she has enjoyed in her experience with childbirth and returning to work as been because of her rank. Specifically when it comes to pushing for policies to apply to them that are not as straightforward as maternity leave (such as breast-feeding), Jane says, most lower-ranking servicewomen will be reluctant to do so, given their position.

I know now a lot of women personally . . . you know, if you're an aircraft mechanic, and you work in a hangar bay, there's not really a decent place to go pump, and while, you know, there—while there's a Marine Corps order that says you have to be given a certain amount of time and a space to do it, most women, you know, lower-ranking females, are not going to push that. They're not going to fight for that—in most cases, they're not going to fight to get a space set aside just for that.

Many of the servicewomen are aware of the complications that these power relationships can present for women claiming their rights and meeting their work/life needs. For that reason, several describe their commitment to keeping an eye out for other servicewomen at lower ranks. Sophia, a twenty-three-year-old with an infant, who is a third-class petty officer in the Navy, says she tries to look out for those mothers around her of lower rank. She says she actively tries to offer support and guidance to those fellow sailors:

I noticed that, you know, I'd try a lot harder to be more of a role model, especially for the really younger girls. Like we have an eighteen-year-old girl in the shop who's pregnant, and newly married and, you know, I try to help steer her and a couple of the others. . . . All of my E-3 and below sailors—and I'm—they're not precisely mine, but I call them mine—all of my E-3 and below sailors in my shop, they all know my address and they all know my phone number, and they all know they have a . . . place to crash anytime they need it.

These relationships represent the third significant theme that Chloe reflects on as having influenced her thinking about rights and her rights claiming. Relationships with both colleagues and supervisors, Chloe explains, can often be crucial. In relating her experiences, Chloe describes meeting active resistance to her desire to continue pumping breast milk for her third child (now four years old) when she was sent overseas six months after giving birth. In a foreign country, housed in a barracks with other servicewomen, Chloe was unable to pump or store her breast milk. "I'm fighting with them over there trying to find space or sanitary places where I can do this—pump and stuff—and it got to the point it was so bad, I threatened them. I was like, 'I'm gonna go congressional!' Somebody needs to protect me—somebody needs to stand up for me.'" Eventually she sought connections with the hospital on base, and, she says, "It was the nurses—the females—who were very sympathetic and made it happen." The nurses, who were in a different branch of the armed forces altogether, made arrangements for Chloe to stay in a room at the hospital, where she was able to pump and store her milk in their break room freezer. "I nearly had a nervous breakdown. That's how upsetting it was for me," says Chloe, who says that without the assistance of the nurses, she would have had to cease breast-feeding against her will. Nevertheless, when Chloe finished her six weeks abroad and was preparing to return home, she was informed that she would not receive an expected decoration for her work there. "And I asked why I didn't get the decoration: 'Well, you threatened to go congressional and that put a bad taste in everybody's mouth.' So it had nothing to do with my performance."

Chloe's experience on her overseas tasking demonstrates the significance of interpersonal relationships. First, positive relationships, like those she created with the Army nurses, can make all the difference in a service member's ability to claim her rights (in Chloe's case, the right to breast-feed at work).[32] Second, Chloe's negative relationships with her commanding officers, generated because she threatened to break the chain of command due to her needs not being met, resulted in her losing an anticipated decoration because she gave people a "bad taste."

Other women, such as Eileen, a thirty-three-year old staff sergeant in the Air Force, describe the salience of their interpersonal relationships for their conceptualization of rights and their ability to claim them. Eileen describes how a woman she worked with who had breast-fed informed her of her right to request space and time to pump at work. When asked whether this woman made the difference to whether she continued breast-feeding when returning to work, Eileen says,

Absolutely. And I felt like I wasn't alone, because there was another woman there. You know, it sounds ridiculous—and 'cause the men were—they were nice, and they were helpful, but you know, sometimes she would say the things I would like to say to those guys on my behalf. You know what I mean? So I wouldn't have to say, "Can I slip away?"

Many of the servicewomen describe the need to band together to counter the masculine culture in the military—and the images of female service members as trying to get out of duty. Gail, a thirty-one-year-old captain in the Marines points out:

> There are very few female Marine officers, only 6 percent of the officer corps is female, and so—which is kind of nice, because we tend to be kind of a close-knit group, but you know, it's also—you have plenty of female officer friends, but only a few of them have children, you know, or—they have children and immediately got out of the Marine Corps because they didn't feel like they could uphold, you know, having a career and having kids.

Brianna, a thirty-four-year-old E-4 in the Army, agrees that female service members often feel the need to band together due to the male-dominated culture surrounding them:

> There's a lot of male counterparts that don't know squat [about female service members' rights] because they just don't want to learn it. So you have to know it . . . and of course you have, you know, like smoke pit lawyers [colleagues who share information about regulations and norms in order to try to assist each other in navigating what is often a difficult workplace culture] that are, like, oh did you hear about this, and did you hear about that? So you know everybody starts to Google it and try to find new regulations or whatever.

In these examples, it is possible to see how servicewomen rely on networking in strategic ways. Such networks do not simply supply information and support, but often reflect a shared experience with and desire to resist a male-dominated culture in their workplace. Much like the academic women, servicewomen seem to rely on each other a great deal for legal knowledge about their workplace—both in terms of sharing and interpreting the formal regulations to which they are entitled, but also in understanding and navigating its informal norms and culture.

Conclusion

Distinguishing the formal and the informal levels within which women must navigate their rights to work/life policies in the workplace sheds light on some of the important ways in which a gap exists between the law on the books and the law in action. The inextricability of the formal from the informal is evident, as women who have claimed their rights formally find that informal consequences await. It is possible to see how servicewomen's thinking about their rights and their decision making about rights are affected by the formal and informal structures surrounding them.

The salience of rank, of an ideal worker norm, and of relationships or professional networks is equally perceptible in this workplace as they are in the public universities in Chapter 1. Where these two institutions seem to differ most significantly is in the actual policies that are in place—and the clarity (or lack of clarity) that results in women's rights consciousness as a result. The significance of this difference will be discussed in more detail in chapter 4 as I probe the institutional factors that affect women's rights consciousness and rights claiming.

3

Looking Out and Speaking Up: Individual Agency and Networks

Eileen is a thirty-three-year-old staff sergeant in the Air Force. She has one preschool-age child and was expecting her second child at the time of our interview. Returning to work after the birth of her first child, Eileen opted to try to breast-feed. She soon discovered, though, that breast-feeding in the Air Force would not be easy. "I didn't really have—there wasn't a lot of support for breast-feeding, so I actually built a—like a tent—in the warehouse where I worked, because I was transportation . . . and I would pump in there." Eileen credits her ability to arrange this setup, and to follow through with her choice to continue breast-feeding with the support and encouragement of an older female colleague. "There was one older female military person who also breast-fed, and so she taught me tips, and she said, these are your rights—that you're allowed to go do this . . . that encouraged me to think I could do it, you know?"

Eileen says that this colleague, who was her senior in both age and rank, shared stories about how difficult it had been for her having a baby and breast-feeding years earlier.

I feel very lucky she was there when I was there. . . . She had two kids, and she was able to still do twenty years in the service. So to know that she was able to get through that—and she had it a lot harder than I did. I mean, she would tell me stories of, you know, when she gave birth, they said, well just put the—a playpen next to your desk, we still need you to come into work. [Laughs] You're kidding me! I just gave birth, I'm not coming to work, and they would just, you know, they would put her—she was a [civil engineer], so she did everything from, like, inspections and—she would be where carcinogens were and hazardous material, and they just didn't care, she was a woman in CE, and there's not a lot of women in CE, certainly as you get higher in the ranks and, um, they really treated her bad. So she would kind of say you know—she would tell me her stories, and then maybe I wouldn't feel so bad that I actually had it pretty good. . . . [She] helped me write a waiver that would help me to just wear my ABUs [airman battle uniform, which would be more comfortable postpartum than a dress uniform] for a few months . . . you know, little things like that. . . . I felt like I had someone helping me."

Eileen's story illustrates the constitutive power of interaction. In connecting with her senior colleague, Eileen attests that she was able to accomplish more to claim her rights in the workplace than she would otherwise have alone. In this and the next two chapters, I analyze my comparative interview data in light of each thread of the theoretical framework that affects legal consciousness formation. I begin this chapter by looking specifically at the role that individuals play as agents of their own legal consciousness formation. Individuals gain their knowledge and develop their thinking about the law from institutional norms and structures,[1] picking up on and perpetuating ideologies that are prevalent in public discourse,[2] and personal experiences with the law.[3] In this chapter, I spend some time exploring the dimension in which social interaction affects legal consciousness formation—instrumental design. Specifically, I introduce and develop a theory of how individuals strategically interact with others within institutional settings in order to instrumentally affect their own legal consciousness and the legal consciousness of others around them. Much like Eileen, many of the other women in this study reflect on their interactions with others as they discuss the ways in which they have come to think about their legal environments and make decisions about rights claiming.

In *Distorting the Law*, Haltom and McCann discuss instrumental design largely in the context of individual elites, who strategically seek to alter public discourse regarding tort reform to bend to their own political and ideological objectives.[4] While this is the particular context for their analysis of the instrumental design element of their framework, I do not believe that instrumental design need only apply to elites. Rather, instrumental design is simply the individual dimension of these interwoven processes, and the notion of design indicates that an element of agency is important to understanding how legal consciousness is formed.

As we have seen, women in both public universities and the U.S. military were taking part in a kind of informal networking process that affected the formation of their legal consciousness. This networking appears to have served not only to inform their legal knowledge but was sometimes also effective in providing emotional and professional support and in improving their likelihood of perceiving success in claiming their rights. In this chapter, I develop more fully a theory of how individuals intentionally seek to influence their own legal consciousness and the legal consciousness of those around them within a particular institutional and policy context. I argue that the phenomenon of institutional consciousness networks is one that has been hitherto largely overlooked in law and society scholarship. Yet it is a phenomenon that, once better understood, can inform future research on legal consciousness formation and offer important signposts for policymakers in thinking about how to effect social change within institutions.

Theorizing Strategic Consciousness Networks

Internal organizational norms and processes can shape the discourse around rights and outcomes for rights claims in a significant way[5] and create substantial obstacles to individuals who might want to claim their rights.[6] Edelman and Suchman observe that organizations are involved in a three-fold process of shaping understandings of the law through facilitative, regulatory, and constitutive legal environments that not only have an impact on individual legal consciousness but are also part of an endogenous process of constructing law itself.[7] As Edelman puts it, "The state may help to constitute organizations through legal definitions of corporations, shareholders, and employees. But the constitutive environment is shaped more by organizational institutions than by the pens of legislators."[8] Workplaces as organizations therefore provide a context in which workers develop their legal consciousness concerning legislation that applies to their workplace identities—and especially that legislation which must be implemented and executed within the space of the workplace. Furthermore, individuals interact within these institutional contexts—with both the institutional structures themselves, as well as other individuals. This interaction is an important part of the production of legal consciousness, as individuals simultaneously both interpret and participate in the construction of their legal environment.

Institutions are clearly important providers of context; they are an important source that these women draw on to develop their legal consciousness. I conceive of institutional consciousness networks (ICNs) as being both part of an institutional context and also distinct from it. As we have seen in Chapters 1 and 2 (and as will become clear in the discussion later in this chapter), an important quality of the networks that women formed within these institutional case studies is that they are institution specific. Indeed, this institution-specific nature differentiates ICNs in these cases from general public discourse. ICNs are generally not made with family members or friends outside work, although women do seem to be speaking to these individuals for support and information. One of the things that differentiates an ICN from, say, a network of family and friends is that this network is able to offer institution-specific information, advocacy, and sites where resistance to institution-specific norms or policies can be voiced. After all, if a woman in the Air Force were speaking with a tenure-track faculty member at an academic institution, these women might indeed be able to provide emotional support for one another as working mothers. But the legal knowledge, support, and resistance to institution-specific norms or policies are unique to the intrainstitutional ICNs that women developed in their respective cases. In other words, the *legal consciousness-building* function of such a network depends on its *institutional specificity* in order to be of the greatest effectiveness for the women using it within their specific, legal environment.

Though this connection to institutions is important to defining an ICN, these networks must also be understood as necessarily distinct from institutions as well. These networks exist within and are influenced by institutional norms, cultures, policies, and structures but are informal networks that are not institutionally directed or created. Influenced by institutional context, ICNs provide a separate source of influence on individual legal consciousness, since they are sources of information (and misinformation) regarding institutions and how to navigate rights claiming in them; they are also sources of support from and resistance to the institutional context as well. Therefore, while ICNs may at times reproduce and reinforce institutional contexts, they can also be sites for resistance to these contexts. Furthermore, ICNs are perhaps the best means of observing how individuals may act with agency to shape the legal environment of their institutions.

While my specific use of the term *institutional consciousness networks* and the definition I derive using my interview data is unique to this study, scholars of social movements, law and society, and institutions have picked up on the informal yet intentional connections that individuals make within institutional settings in various ways. Catherine Albiston, for instance, in studying how individuals choose to claim their rights to FMLA, recognizes that individuals make strategic connections, and that these connections help shape individuals' consciousness and rights mobilization:

Respondents in this study indicated that the existence of legal rights prompted them to talk with others about their experiences in the workplace, to discuss whether their employers' actions were legitimate, and in some instances, to band together to resist their employer's reinterpretation of family and medical leave. In this sense, then, informal rights mobilization can be understood as a social, rather than individual, process of meaning construction as well as action.[9]

Similarly, Elizabeth Hirsch and Christopher Lyons document the importance of what they identify as workplace relationships in helping to form a higher degree of racial consciousness and perceptions of discrimination among nonwhite workers:

> The increase in racial group identification and cohesion afforded by numbers makes discrimination a more accessible social construct for understanding negative events. . . . The process of identifying experiences as discrimination is embedded in a larger workplace context and set of relations that influence the likelihood of naming, and subsequently reporting, discrimination.[10]

Several scholars have observed that such informal institutional relationships, networks, or connections are particularly important when allowing individuals who desire to express resistance to connect with others wishing to do the same. Ewick and Silbey, for example, argue that telling stories of resistance may lay the foundation for more organized collective action: "The narrative structure of these anecdotes suggests, if nothing else, that these stories had been told before to friends, acquaintances, coworkers, and family. In fact, sharing stories of resistance may be one means through which individual encounters with power become the basis for collective action."[11]

Karen Brodkin Sacks, in documenting the process of organization to collective action among Black women hospital workers, traces how women's friendships and informal networking among coworkers led to more formal organizing. In this way, Sacks clearly connects ICNs with more formal collective action—with ICNs serving as the potential foundation for such mobilization.[12] More recently, Katherine Kellogg has found that what she calls "relational spaces"—places where reformers can comfortably talk and develop strategies of resistance to the status quo—can help to develop what she calls "relational efficacy" among reformers.[13] This again emphasizes the importance of more informal connections in the workplace as providing the building blocks for more formalized collective action.

Significantly, though, ICNs are used not only as ways for individuals to voice resistance. They are also sources of information and support. Such a combination of functions means that they have the potential to affect women's legal consciousness in multiple ways and are also important in their decision making when it comes to rights mobilization. This is yet another way in which these networks might be seen as intentional or as the result of agency. Individuals may actively seek out these networks as a means of deepening their own legal consciousness and affecting the legal consciousness of those around them. Phoebe Morgan documents the importance of relational connections for women's rights consciousness—and their decisions to mobilize their rights or not—in the area of sexual harassment.[14] What is interesting to note about Morgan's study, however, in contrast to this one, is that for Morgan's subjects, the most significant relationships for the development of their rights consciousness and decision to mobilize or not are *familial*. In contrast, women in this study are citing relationships within their *workplace* as significant to their perceptions about institutional norms and their ability to claim rights within these contexts.

This contrast highlights another important point. ICNs, as they are formed in these cases, are phenomena that may depend in large part on the nature of work/family law and policy itself. In other words, something about the work/family laws and policies (as opposed to, for example, sexual harassment policy) means that women are more likely to reach out to others in their workplace to form significant ICNs. A number of possible explanations for this come to mind. For instance, there is a relative lack of stigma for claiming something like maternity leave versus accusing someone of sexual harassment. Additionally, many more women who have claimed these policies are likely to be present in the workplace, as compared with other types of policies. One could also imagine, however, other policies where such institution-specific, consciousness-building connections may be important to make, and thus might be important areas of future study on the existence and function of ICNs. For instance, hour and wage, workplace safety, and health care policies may all be areas with lower levels of associated stigma (compared with sexual harassment or discrimination policies), and with which a higher number of employees have engaged.

Institutional consciousness networks are loose, informal connections among actors within a workplace, created for the purposes of navigating workplace norms and policies more effectively. These connections are sometimes formed through actual relationships (or friendships) between individuals and sometimes only through acquaintance and observation. These connections can be horizontal (among peers) or vertical (across ranks in a hierarchical structure). These networks are intentional, workplace specific, and, importantly, can offer those in these networks professional advantages. Moreover, they are networks of "consciousness," where members gain and share a degree of knowledge of and experience with the law, and this consciousness in turn shapes individuals' decision-making processes within their legal environments. It is within these networks that we can observe individuals acting with agency within their specific institutional settings in order to shape their own legal consciousness and also to have an impact on the legal environment—and legal consciousness—of others within the institution.

Institutional Consciousness Networks in Action

In speaking with women faculty members and servicewomen, I detected three distinct patterns in the ways that institutional consciousness networks seem to influence these women's legal consciousness. First, ICNs offer information, which builds individuals' legal knowledge and understanding of their formal rights, as well as the informal norms that are often just as important to understand and navigate in order to rights-claim. Second, these networks offer emotional and professional support for women. Some women credit this support with motivating them to claim their rights, where they might otherwise have not mobilized, or to stay in their job, where they might otherwise have been tempted to quit. Finally, these networks can focus collective resistance to institutional policies or norms.

Providing Legal Knowledge

In both institutional cases, women described turning to other mothers in their workplace for information and education. The kind of information women sought varied according to their individual and institutional needs, but generally they sought information about both the formal policies available to them and informal norms in their workplace and how to navigate them. At Elm University, Carol, a thirty-nine-year-old associate professor, says, "I turn to my—my professional friends, my friends who are also faculty who have kids—I turn to them for so much. You know, they are my number one resource, I would say, in terms of just information." Kay, a thirty-two-year-old assistant professor at Elm who is thinking about having children, agrees that asking other women is where she would begin to gain knowledge about her rights. "So what I would start by doing is like asking all my friends, you know, what's the policy in place."

Several women recounted going to colleagues first for information and clarification of the policies in place at their respective institutions. Lyla, a forty-five-year-old assistant professor at Oak University, says that a colleague who was pregnant at the same time she was engaged her in conversations about university policies on several occasions. Lyla says that, importantly, "she and I spent a lot of time talking, and she's the one who turned me on to the person in human resources that was my big advocate." This HR contact eventually was instrumental in helping Lyla claim her right to stop her tenure clock, even though she submitted her paperwork to do so late, because, says Lyla, an interim department chair had not explained the policy well enough to her. Taylor, a thirty-eight-year-old assistant professor at Oak, also credits conversations with other mothers with providing her with important legal knowledge. Being from another country, Taylor says that she "wasn't aware of their policy" when she first became pregnant at Oak and was "naive" about what she would be entitled to. She became pregnant at the time that Oak University was negotiating with its faculty union to implement its paid family leave policy, and she says that her colleague provided her with a lot of information about the process since it would inevitably affect her. "I have a friend . . . who has a son who is twelve days older than my daughter and she's on the faculty senate, so she kept sending me updates about what was happening with family leave."

Constance, an assistant professor at Elm, says that she sought out other mothers in her department before speaking to her chair directly about her pregnancy because she wanted to gain an understanding about the informal norms of her department regarding pregnancy and work. She wanted to know what to expect when speaking to her supervisor, what the atmosphere in the department was toward new parents, and what strategies she should use in speaking with him. Constance says, "I asked some of the other female faculty in the department what I should do and how I should handle it. And they said, just tell him—and tell him the baby's coming in June, and it won't affect your teaching, and you know he's really great; don't worry about it."

While many of the women interviewed describe having sought out friends for information, developing relationships is not a necessary aspect of strategic consciousness networks. Some women in the academic institution, for instance, did not learn about the informal norms in their department through relationships but through observations of other women. Paige, for example, a forty-nine-year-old associate professor at Oak University, says that she had a colleague approach her to tell her that observing her experience had had a significant impact on her decision making:

One woman . . . said to me, "You've shown me how to do it. You know, you've shown me that it's doable." . . . And I had no awareness that I was doing that, you know; I had none whatsoever, but for some reason, just seeing me do it sort of helped her concretely imagine this possibility, which I just think is great, you know—like, in the most sort of mechanical sense of cognitive priming . . . as opposed to actual mentorship.

In the U.S. military, the institutional structure of the maternity/convalescent leave policy means that the information that women seek from their strategic consciousness networks is somewhat different. As was detailed in Chapter 1, women faculty members are often entitled to very different maternity leave policies (depending on their institution, rank, and time of service). In contrast, as I explained in Chapter 2, at the time of these interviews, all women in the military were granted a minimum of six weeks of paid leave.[15] "I guess it's just expected that a mom's going to get so much maternity leave," says Natalie, a thirty-nine-year-old Air Force major. Natalie's relationships with other mothers in the civilian world are her source of information for what other workplaces offer. She describes how these networks inform her consciousness of how her rights under her workplace policies compare with those elsewhere and cause her to feel content with the policies available to her: "I've heard that . . . some people have to save up their paid time to be able to use that during their time off, or some people have to take it without pay, which to me would probably cause some people to come back to work sooner. " Natalie says that because postpartum leave is such a given in the military, it is just the perceived extras that servicewomen feel the need to network with each other to learn about: "I guess it's just the amount of time that people talk about. Are they going to take extra time? Is that going to impact everybody else in the job because they want to take extra time?" Indeed, extra time, as well as whether to breast-feed, and how to go about requesting policies that are not seen as being so routine, seem to be where servicewomen most often seek out ICNs for information on formal policies and informal norms.

Despite the apparently straightforward nature of maternity leave in the U.S. military, more minor aspects of pregnancy and returning to work can be tricky to navigate, such as gaining permission to reduce hours, change duties or uniforms when pregnant, or get space and time to breast-feed when returning to work. Penny, a twenty-four-year-old former enlisted member of the Navy, says that talking with other women who have been through a pregnancy in the military is important, even for women who know what leave they are entitled to. It can be confusing to navigate the paperwork, special instructions, and other minor details without any guidance.

I feel like with the Navy it's a lot of—probably with all of the branches of the military—it's a lot of runaround, and you kind of have to figure out things as you go along. But . . . I was good friends with a couple people, and they had been through it, so they knew what I had to do, so I basically talked to them.

By speaking to her friends who had already been through the process of claiming their rights under Navy regulations covering pregnancy, Penny found out that she was able to have her hours reduced toward the end of her pregnancy and change her combat boots for sneakers. These are both accommodations that most of the servicewomen in this study were eligible to claim, but some chose not to or did not realize that they were entitled to. Penny credits her friends' advice with her knowledge of and success in claiming these accommodations.

Breast-feeding on returning to work is another area where servicewomen sought counsel and information from ICNs with other servicewomen who had experience with claiming their rights. As we saw, Eileen credits a senior colleague with helping her to learn what formal rights she was entitled to in the Air Force with regard to breast-feeding: "She taught me, you know, tips, and she said these are your rights that, you know, you're allowed to go do this, and she showed me the AFIs [Air Force Instruction]."[16]

Legal knowledge is an important component of rights consciousness. If individuals are to make choices about rights mobilization—indeed, if they are to think about themselves as rights holders—then the necessary first step in that activation process is gaining some knowledge of one's rights. ICNs are one way that individuals are able to obtain legal knowledge, or pass on legal knowledge to others, in a way that is inherently instrumental. Individuals act as agents of their own legal knowledge formation (and in helping to inform the legal knowledge of others), and thus actively participate in constructing this aspect of legal consciousness.

Providing Emotional and Professional Support

Many of the servicewomen interviewed talked at length about their experiences with fellow servicewomen who stood up for them, mentored them, or offered them emotional or professional support. To be clear, emotional support in the context of ICNs is not solely for the purposes of making individuals within the network feel warm and fuzzy, though that may be an effect of this support. The key component of the support that these networks offer—what makes them useful within the institutional setting of the workplace—is that they provide a professional boost.

Perhaps due to the military ethos of looking out for one another, the military case seemed to be a particularly good source for discovering the importance of emotional and professional support produced by strategic consciousness networks. Several of the servicewomen described other men and women advocating on their behalf or themselves acting as advocates for other service members. Kelly, a forty-five-year-old Army sergeant first class with two children, says that many offices on her base are places where families feel comfortable helping each other out. She describes colleagues picking up each other's children and others bringing their children into the office on occasion. "I mean it's just—the military's one huge family for the most part. Do we all talk about our children? Absolutely."

As detailed in Chapter 2, several women discussed the significance of other servicewomen advocating on their behalf. Chloe, for instance, said that Army nurses' assisting her with expressing and storing breast milk while on a short-term deployment meant that she was not forced to cease breast-feeding early. Gail, a captain in the Marines, also pointed out that this advocacy and support was particularly important for women in the officer corps because of their smaller numbers.

In addition to horizontal professional support, however, servicewomen seemed to also benefit a great deal from emotional and professional support vertically or across ranks—from both women and from men. Several women described supportive supervisors, who looked out for them during pregnancy and when they returned to work. Eileen, for instance, said that a higher-ranking colleague in the Air Force stood up for her on a number of occasions with her male colleagues when she needed to slip away from the office to breast-feed. Emma, a twenty-eight-year-old enlisted Marine, also describes being enthusiastically supported by her supervisor. She says that her immediate supervisor's wife had a child around the same time as she did, and that both her supervisor and his wife were in the hospital the day after she had given birth. "He took care of all the paperwork, right then and there" so that she didn't have to report to her base to do so. In addition, she describes him as "jumping through hoops to accommodate for me."

Other women also described actively advocating on behalf of their subordinates. Gabrielle, for instance, a thirty-six-year-old lieutenant colonel in the Air Force with two children, says that her status as an officer and as a mother means that women are always seeking her out for advice and support, and she is always ready to give it: "When folks do seek you out for your opinion or, 'Hey how did you manage this?' or 'How did you do that?'—I always make myself available for that. . . . I try never to be judgmental." Service members of lower ranks, such as Sophia, a third-class petty officer in the Navy, also discussed actively looking out for subordinates who were pregnant and in need of advice or assistance.

Women faculty members at both public universities also used ICNs to give and receive similar forms of emotional and professional support. Eve, a thirty-three-year-old assistant professor at Elm University, explains that many women who are in tenured or tenure-track position at the university have formed an informal network, where women offer advice on how best to navigate the modification-of-duties policy. Eve says that other faculty members are often pointed to her to ask for advice on applying for the policy, and she has done so twice. "I think it's just word-of-mouth. I think . . . we kind of network together. Or people have just pointed in my direction. We're a relatively small campus; even for as large as we are, it's a small community. And I think it's just word-of-mouth." Carol, in particular, also often finds herself at the center of a network that helps faculty claim modification of duties for the first time. She notes that in recent years, this process has become harder for women at the university:

God these days, those kinds of conversations are like, "How am I gonna get a decent modification of duties?" And um, and the answer is, "I don't know." Like, what I've been hearing . . . essentially, people submit a modification proposal, and it gets bounced back—you need to do more work. And they submit it with more work, and it gets bounced back. No, you need to do more work."

More and more, says Carol, women are turning to other women who have undergone the process for help and advice on how to have their proposal accepted. Barbara, for instance, a thirty-six-year-old assistant professor at Elm, says that networking with other colleagues who had undergone the modification-of-duties application significantly helped her to develop a successful plan of her own:

The people who were particularly helpful were three of the colleagues who had done the modified duties prior to me, so I was able—they sent me their plans, and I was able to look at them and then . . . one of them in particular—I sent her my rough draft, and she made comments about what I should change and so, in that process, I was able to get it really refined, and then when I sent it to the appropriate people from there, it got accepted without any changes needing to be made.

Where military servicewomen and academic women seem to diverge most strikingly in their use of ICNs is in the degree to which emotional and professional support is given across ranks. Institutional hierarchies and rank are salient in both public universities and the U.S. military, and these institutional factors have significant effects on how women make decisions regarding their rights. ICNs are simply another element of legal consciousness formation where rank is salient for women in both academia and the military. As I discuss in more depth in the next chapter, rights claiming is harder for those at the bottom of the ladder, and higher ranks correspond with greater opportunities for rights-claiming.

Given the degree of professional support exhibited by servicewomen, one would expect a similar function for ICNs in public universities. However, the emotional and professional support that took place through ICNs at the public universities in this study was more closely connected with rank than those in the U.S. military. While professors, associate professors, and assistant professors were all entitled to the modified-duties policy at Elm University or the paid leave policy at Oak University, contingent faculty, such as visiting assistant professors and adjunct faculty, at the public universities were not entitled to the same policies as their tenured or tenure-track colleagues. Tenured or tenure-track faculty rarely made mention of this difference in the way that policies applied across ranks at their institutions, and none said that they had taken any action to advocate for changing this. But visiting faculty and adjuncts felt this distinction keenly and repeatedly mentioned feeling a lack of professional support in this area from other faculty members. Valerie, a thirty-one-year-old visiting assistant professor at Elm, is the most vocal about this. She says that she felt that her department chair and other faculty in her department had been supportive when she got pregnant, but that the support had seemed hollow in that it had not been useful to her professionally:

I think that the chair of my department said something like, you know, "Okay, I really encourage you, I really think kids are great, you should plan to have as many kids as you know as you possibly want, that's really awesome and I'd be supportive of you making that a goal in your life," or something like that. He didn't say *and* [emphasis hers] I'll go and fight for you on the faculty senate committee about this policy that I consider to be full of shit. So it was supportive . . . but it didn't go as far as, in an ideal world, as I think it could.

Valerie is so fed up with what she perceives as the lack of support for mothers in academia that she has decided not to pursue a tenure-track career. Her experience of a lack of mentorship and professional support has had an impact on her career choices. She discusses the lack of women at the top ranks of academia as a failure of both policy and mentorship:

I think that women see these policies and they're like, "Screw it"—like, "I don't want that job," and then they're all leaving. And then—so the girls who are in grad school . . . all of my mentors in grad school were male. And none of them were like, "Hey, it sucks to be a woman in tenure," like "Have you thought about that?" Because I don't think they had that experience. I don't think they knew.

The lack of professional support across these ranks in the public universities in this study does not mean that professional support is not a key component of ICNs. Rather, that Valerie and others like her *sought* these types of connections but were not able to find them speaks to the important work that ICNs can do when they are present and the significant impact that their absence has not only on individuals' legal consciousness but also on their professional opportunities.

ICNs are not simply ways for individuals to gain legal knowledge; they also play a crucial role in how individuals interpret their rights and their relationship to them. An individual such as Valerie may possess legal knowledge and yet still feel demobilized when it comes to rights claiming. Valerie sometimes frames this difficulty with accessing the full benefits available to her tenure-track colleagues as a choice. At other times, she acknowledges that were she to have better support from her colleagues, she might be better able to access rights that others take for granted. In this way, ICNs offer more than legal knowledge; they are also a tool that women use to help interpret their social positioning as rights holders and potential rights claimers. ICNs can *enable* rights claims by providing professional or emotional support in assisting women to rights-claim. As Valerie's story demonstrates, however, when ICNs do not provide such support, women still use these networks to help interpret and make meaning of rights within their legal environment.

Providing the Building Blocks for Organized Resistance

Women across both institutions use ICNs as a source of legal knowledge and, often, as a tool for supporting rights mobilization.

In some cases, however, these ICNs play a more active role in providing individuals an outlet for their resistance to policies or norms that are collectively seen as unfair. To be clear, ICNs in this role are not yet organized resistance; they are not unions or mobilized interest groups of any kind. Rather, institutional consciousness networks can form the foundation for such collective action by bringing individuals together in a looser, more informal way that later may take a more organized shape. ICNs may be thought of as a kind of primordial soup with the potential to develop into more formal collective action.

An excellent example of ICNs performing this "resistance" function is evident in the backroom talk among faculty mothers at Elm University, particularly surrounding the modification-of-duties policy. Many of the faculty interviewed felt that the provost's office at Elm had been unfair or inconsistent in how it was approving plans to modify workloads. Charlotte, for instance, a thirty-five-year-old assistant professor with a young child, says that she has been disturbed by the inconsistencies in how the policy is being applied across campus—inconsistencies that she has heard about through her ICN. She says these reports make her nervous about timing the birth of her next child:

It also seems to vary in terms of the modified duties as to what you can get depending on when you are due. So, I don't know who else you've talked to at the college, but—so we have two women in the department that were— that gave birth in November and they got relief of their teaching duties in the spring, so they didn't come back until August, so that's almost a full year. Then we have one right now who gave birth in April or May and has the fall off or modified duties and won't come back until January, but then we have others who come back, you know, a lot sooner. So I think it— sometimes it depends on the actual timing of the birth, which I'm kind of curious about. Compared with others across campus—I have a colleague in another department whose department chair was trying to get her to teach an express class [a course that meets for fewer weeks but for longer periods of time], which would basically start like the day after her FMLA ends. . . . I guess as someone who feels like I want to contribute to the college beyond my department . . . something about that feels kind of unfair, I guess.

Charlotte says that many other faculty members that she has spoken to share her perception of this unfairness, and the interview data bear this out. Alex, a thirty-five-year-old mother of two, who is an associate professor, says that she was very happy with her own modification-of-duties plan but that hearing recently of a colleague's struggles with the policy has angered her and made her fearful for the next time she will need to use it. Alex gets emotional when talking about the fact that a friend and colleague of hers was required to teach a new class when she returned to work after her maternity leave, and thus was not able to modify her duties to exclude teaching for that semester, as Alex had been able to. "Up until [my colleague's] deal, I would have sung praises about the process. . . . But when I see something like that happen, it just—it's like, well then why is there not a standard policy across the campus?"

This widespread sense of unfairness—and, more important, the discussion of this sense of unfairness among women who are networking to help each other with their applications for the modification-of-duties policy—has developed into a kind of loose network of resistance to the policy. Nora, the forty-eight-year-old associate professor at Elm who was introduced in Chapter 1, described "backroom talk" that was taking place at Elm among female faculty about how best to get around the policy's requirements so as to get the "best deal."

Military servicewomen also seem to use ICNs as a means of resisting—though unlike the women faculty members, this resistance focuses on informal norms that exist in the military rather than formal policy. As Gail, a thirty-one-year-old captain in the Marines pointed out earlier, the heavily male-dominated nature of the military often causes women to come together to resist what can often be perceived as a misogynistic culture. Brianna, a thirty-four-year-old enlisted soldier in the Army, agrees that female service members often feel the need to band together due to the male-dominated culture surrounding them. This leads to a rise in what Brianna calls "smoke pit lawyers"—colleagues who share information about regulations and norms in order to try to assist each other in navigating what is often a difficult workplace culture. Servicewomen rely on ICNs not simply for information and support but often connect with one another out of a shared experience with and desire to resist a male-dominated culture in their workplace.

Sometimes resistance to this culture means servicewomen publicly speak up for their female colleagues. Gina, a thirty-six-year-old mother of two who is a noncommissioned officer in the Coast Guard, says that she has often tried to speak up for her lower-ranking colleagues when others gave them a hard time for being pregnant in the service. "There's a real junior E-4 who I've kinda kept an eye on and just made sure that she was doing okay. . . . Her immediate coworkers are fine, but I've heard other guys in the office giving her shit about, you know, taking time to get her pump, and stuff like that. It drives me crazy. So, you know, I always speak up when I hear it." Liv, a twenty-six-year-old enlisted Army soldier says that she remembers a female colleague speaking up for her in a similar way: "Somebody said, 'You know, [Liv] just got pregnant to get out of the deployment,' and [my colleague] said, 'No she didn't; she just got back.'" In this case, Liv's colleague helped her to resist a common stereotype that military servicewomen who become pregnant must often face: that they got pregnant in order to "get out of" deploying overseas. By standing up for her, Liv's colleague actively challenged this stereotype on Liv's behalf.

Within both the public universities and the U.S. military, ICNs are informal groupings of men and women. These groupings are so loose at times that an actual relationship is not always necessary. For this reason, these networks cannot perform the same functions as more formalized collective action. However, these networks do serve a crucial role in making individuals aware of themselves as members of a group. Individuals who even simply observe others like them claiming rights can become "activated."[17] They perceive that they are part of a group and that this group is entitled to rights—whether they are formal, codified rights or more amorphous "rights" to be treated in a particular way. Such group consciousness is the foundation for more organized group action.

Conclusion

Institutional consciousness networks, as demonstrated in these cases, are sometimes formed through relationships and sometimes not. They are sometimes used to gather information, sometimes to gain emotional and professional support, and sometimes as a way to share a common desire to resist policy or cultures surrounding policies in a workplace. While not uniform in their impact, it is clear from these interviews that ICNs can have an important effect on individuals' rights consciousness and rights mobilization.

In her book *Talking about Politics: Informal Groups and Social Identity in American Life*, Katherine Cramer Walsh makes an important observation that "public discussion" is something that scholars tend to assume takes place among "political professionals"—that political elites, the mass media, and interest groups are where individuals primarily derive their ideas about politics and their political understanding.[18] Walsh argues that in fact, scholars should not overlook the significance of informal interactions in shaping individuals' ideas and knowledge about politics, and she provides some excellent in-depth ethnographic evidence of the power that informal interactions have in shaping political consciousness. Before Walsh, Melissa Harris-Lacewell also tied the formation of group identity and ideology within Black communities in America to the everyday interactions that individuals had with each other in social spaces such as church or the local barbershop.[19]

Identity and political ideology are both dynamic constructs that require social interaction for their formation, and these scholars highlight the importance of informal social networks in their development. So, too, legal consciousness requires social input. However, what that social input looks like is a conversation that perhaps needs to be more finely tuned in law and society scholarship. My observation of institutional consciousness networks and their role in shaping women's legal consciousness in this particular area of policy strongly suggests that law and society scholars should focus more closely on the significance of informal interactions in shaping legal consciousness. Scholars of institutional change, social movements, and public opinion formation in American politics, and indeed law and society research, have all touched on the significance of these informal social interactions, but the work of scholars such as Walsh suggests that this emphasis needs to be intensified. This book goes one step further in identifying how ICNs function in workplace contexts and how these networks affect the legal consciousness of women in public universities and the U.S. military.

4

Status Speaks: The Importance of Rank

"All right, I started the whole thing late," says Paige, a forty-nine-year-old associate professor at Oak University with two school-age children. "I think I was thirty-two or thirty-three when I started my job. . . . I just had never sort of thought about having kids, but then life events—frankly, death of family members in my thirties, changed my mind." Despite this change in her family plans and her late start, Paige says that she had always planned to delay having children until after receiving tenure. "I wasn't going to try to have kids before tenure, because I just didn't feel secure." Paige felt particularly afraid of losing her job, which provided benefits for her and her husband. "I just literally didn't know if I would get tenure or not, and if I had had a baby and didn't get tenure, then what would we do . . . how would we take care of a . . . pediatrician?"

Paige goes on to describe the tenure process as tenuous and often frightening. "Even if you're doing fine, it's such a hazing process, even in a relatively civilized environment. I mean, I see my junior colleagues, and I mean they're publishing books, they're doing great, and they still have that haunted look because it is—it's a hazing thing." When thinking about the effect of having children on achieving a higher rank within her institution, Paige reflects on the experience of one of her colleagues at another institution: "I have had a friend whose first project . . . looked fine. And then she had the baby, and then somehow they started having doubts about the project."

Paige is not alone in considering the significance of institutional structures such as rank and tenure when navigating her institutional norms and trying to make decisions about claiming her rights to work/life balance policies. This chapter examines more closely the institutional structures of public universities and the U.S. military. It briefly explains how I conceive of institutions and the role that they play in social change and stability. I discuss how the framework of discursive institutionalism allows me to distinguish institutional context from individual agency in a way that is useful for analyzing the processes that govern how ideas are transmitted and internalized within institutional settings. I focus here on how both formal and informal institutional structures operate in transmitting ideas and save a more thorough discussion of which particular ideas are salient in this process for the next chapter.

This chapter details how the interview participants themselves feel that the institutions in which they work structure their thinking and decision making about work/life balance policies. These women's personal narratives illuminate the degree to which institutional factors have affected their rights consciousness and rights claiming. Focusing on one institutional structure—institutional hierarchy, or rank—will allow a more precise look at how institutions and individuals interact in a recursive process that forms individuals' legal consciousness.

The comparative analysis of two case studies provides insight into the institutional impact on rights consciousness formation. The comparative institutional perspective sheds greater light on how institutions work to shape rights consciousness and sets up further discussion of the role ideas play in institutional settings.

Institutions as Discursive Sites

Scholars of new institutionalism, a fairly recent and important turn in social science research that emphasizes the significance of institutional development, organization, composition, and so on, have acknowledged the impact that institutional rules, norms, and structures have on individual decision making.[1] Sociological institutionalism is engaged in explaining organization through cultural norms and frames that give shape to institutions and that institutions in turn serve to perpetuate and disseminate. Institutions are the context in which a logic of appropriateness, dictated by cultural norms and frames, constrains and constructs individual and collective action.[2] Many law and society scholars who focus on the significance of institutions have reflected an understanding of institutions that is largely constructivist and in line with sociological institutionalism.[3]

Discursive institutionalism builds on this conception of institutions in one important way. It introduces the study of the circulation of ideas as a central feature of its analysis. Scholars of this approach argue that institutions

are not external, rule-following structures that serve primarily as constraints on actors. . . . They are instead simultaneously constraining structures and enabling constructs internal to "sentient" (thinking and speaking agents) agents whose "background ideational abilities" explain how they create and maintain institutions at the same time that their "foreground discursive abilities" enable them to communicate critically about those institutions, to change (or maintain) them.[4]

Discursive institutionalism should be particularly attractive to scholars who are interested in better understanding institutions and their role in social change. Its emphasis on the significance of ideas and their communication makes discursive institutionalism an excellent framework with which to explain change and continuity, through the discursive interaction between individual and social within institutional settings. Indeed, as Teresa Kulawik argues, discursive institutionalism allows scholars to view institutions not simply as "sedimentations of discursive struggles."[5] Rather, institutions are also spaces where discourse takes place— and these spaces shape and configure discourse.

Discursive institutionalism focuses on the significance of ideas and how these ideas are communicated within an institutional setting. Institutions are external structures that constrain individuals in the same way that other new institutionalism strains understand them. At the same time, institutions are also constraining and enabling in that these same structures may also be used to communicate critically about the institution and to change it.[6] Discursive institutionalism can be constructivist or positivist, but ultimately it is most often engaged in explaining or demonstrating "the causal influence of ideas and discourse."[7] Discourse does not always matter. Therefore, the important questions for discursive institutionalism are: *when, why,* and *how* do ideas and discourse matter in institutional settings?

Discursive institutionalism offers an important starting point for scholars interested in understanding how rights consciousness is formed in institutional contexts. These scholars are essentially interested in the communication of "rights" as ideas—how rights are interpreted and communicated among individuals and how these ideas then drive rights mobilization. In their edited book, *Institutional Work,* Thomas Lawrence, Roy Suddaby and Bernard Leca argue that the previous work of new institutionalism scholars has understood institutions in terms of how they constrain and govern individual action.[8] Their theory of institutional work (in essence, an attempt to clarify discursive institutionalism scholarship) aims instead to describe a recursive relationship between institutions and individual action. Their analytical focus is on how actors shape institutions. Institutions require actors, and exchanges of ideas between actors, in order to change but also in order to stay the same. Institutional context and individual agency are therefore interwoven concepts that are also distinct in their significance. Individuals operate within institutions and are in a sense the mechanisms that carry out the formal rules and informal norms of institutions. Institutions cannot exist without individual agency, and it is the consensus of individuals that is essentially what constructs an institution to be precisely what it is.[9]

The workplace is understood to be a discursive environment. Individual actors are constrained in their thinking and action by their workplace settings. Individuals can also be enabled by these same structures to change or maintain them through a discursive process of interacting with their institutional setting on a daily basis. Women in both public universities and the U.S. military have been constrained by their workplace contexts in both their rights consciousness and their rights claiming. However, some women in this study have also used their institutional contexts to challenge existing structures. Their involvement in discursive processes within the institutional setting of the workplace provides a key insight into how their understanding of rights in the workplace develops. In addition, an analysis of the discursive interaction between institutions and agency offers greater insights into how rights consciousness is—or is not—put into action within the institution, necessarily affecting the rights consciousness and actions of others within that space.

Discursive Institutions: Evidence from the Case Studies

In relating their experiences with work/life balance policies in their respective workplaces, women in both academia and the U.S. military seem to recognize certain institutional processes and structures as being particularly salient to them. While many of the interview questions asked women to talk about their impressions of multiple facets of their workplaces, I focus closely in this chapter on rank as a salient institutional structure. This focus is by no means meant to deny that individuals, whatever their institutional rank, are actively involved in the construction of institutional norms. Indeed, my discussion of institutional consciousness networks in the previous chapter highlights the ways in which individuals are actively involved in constructing institutional norms and discourses. There are two reasons for this focus on the salience of rank within these institutional settings. First, this institutional structure was most often identified by the women I interviewed as salient in their thinking and decision making regarding their rights at work. Second, examining one aspect of institutional structure more closely makes sense for the purposes of focusing the analysis of the interaction between individuals and institutions. The women interviewed for this study discussed ways in which rank both constrained and enabled their rights claiming.

Institutions as Constraints

Both academic institutions and the various branches of the U.S. military are heavily dependent on hierarchical structures in order to function effectively. While most workplaces in the United States are hierarchically structured, public universities and the military are both institutions that are particularly dependent on such structures. Each institution has a distinct hierarchical structure, where individual women are intuitively aware of the appropriateness of their actions within their respective rank. The consequences of acting in a way that might be deemed inappropriate for one's rank within a hierarchy are real, though they can be complex. Rank is an institutional structure that is codified in both institutions, and certain written rules, rights, and expectations are assigned to various ranks.

In academia, rank is closely tied to obtaining certain benefits. Faculty members at Elm University, for example, are entitled to their university's modified-duties policy only if they are tenured or on the tenure track. Challenging this link between rank and benefits is particularly difficult, since those faculty members with the least power to enact change within the university (contingent faculty) are those who are most interested in changing the policies. As Valerie (a thirty-one-year-old visiting assistant professor at Elm University) has discovered, it is often difficult to persuade those in a position of power granted to them by rank to advocate for those without power. Valerie feels strongly that the variation in policies at Elm across ranks is unfair. Tenured and tenure-track faculty at Elm are entitled to a modification-of-duties policy in the semester following their return from FMLA leave, while visiting faculty are entitled only to FMLA. "I've complained about it to everyone that I've spoken with, you know, very loudly, and they're like, 'Oh well, you know, you should just hope to have a different position.' And I was like, 'Oh right, okay;

it's okay if we screw these people over as long as we're not one of them.'" She goes on to voice her dissatisfaction with the fact that the exclusion seems even more arbitrary in that the policy applies to senior instructors, a position that is technically of a lower rank than a visiting assistant professor. "It's ridiculous," she argues.

This variability of benefit distribution across ranks in academia is constraining not simply in that certain faculty have fewer rights to mobilize. It is also constraining in that the variability makes knowing what rights they are entitled to difficult for most faculty in the academic institutions. Danielle, a thirty-two-year-old visiting assistant professor at Elm who already had one child during the summer months at her institution, said that upon becoming pregnant a second time, she struggled to find out what she would actually be entitled to in terms of maternity leave and said she was shocked to find out that her leave would be unpaid. "So it was a little worrisome, you know, because it's not clear, and nobody could give me a straight answer 'til, like, the very last minute . . . so yeah, that was a scary, scary part." Alex, a thirty-five-year-old associate professor with twins, is also confused by her entitlements at Elm, because she says that not only is the modification-of-duties policy applied differently across ranks, but even among tenured and tenure-track faculty, there seem to be differences in terms of how the policy has been applied. For instance, she was happy with her modified-duties plan, but a friend of hers with a similar standing with the university was given a very different plan, which she was not happy with. Referring to her colleague, Alex says, "Her experience with kid one versus kid two has been different. So I don't think I would get the same deal now as I did then."

In both universities, there was also a consensus that the institutional structure of the tenure track in academia significantly constrains women's rights mobilization in the area of work/life balance because of its coincidental alignment with a woman's fertility clock. The anxiety around this is once again due to the institutional benefits that are tied to certain ranks. Faculty members who are not on the tenure track are presumed to be attempting to become tenure track. Crucially, those on the tenure track are expected to perform a certain number of specified duties (publishing, teaching, and service) within a small window of time (usually five to seven years), before going up for tenure. If tenure is not achieved, the faculty member is often discharged from the university. If tenure is granted, this rank bestows certain privileges on the faculty member—not least of which is a significant easing of the professional duties required to obtain tenure or a period of sabbatical or both. Waiting to have children until achieving tenure is a rational goal for faculty members, primarily because an institution must now have "just cause" in order for a faculty member to have her employment terminated. In other words, she is significantly more secure in her job once reaching the rank of tenured associate professor.

The structure of tenure is meant to liberate faculty to think and work about potentially controversial topics without fear of institutional retribution.[10] Many of the faculty members I interviewed, however, talked about the tenure process as something that is also constraining—primarily to their ability to claim their rights to work/life balance policies before achieving tenure. The prospect of endangering their job security while on the tenure track was particularly frightening for several of these women. As we saw, Paige was so concerned about the effects of having children while she was still in the lower ranks of academia that she waited until she had tenure to have children. Carol, Kay, Nora, and several other faculty women all expressed similar justifications for waiting until they had tenure to have children. "I don't mind waiting, it's just—I feel like it does tie my hand a bit," says Kay, who is waiting until she is tenured to have children.

The fact that rank is not linked with the distribution of policy benefits within the military (as it is in academia) results in some important differences in rights mobilization of maternity leave across the two institutions. As mentioned briefly in Chapter 2, all of the servicewomen interviewed said that they had had no problem with claiming their right to maternity leave in the military. The comparison between the implementation of maternity leave at the two institutions strongly suggests that the universal application of the policy across all ranks has a lot to do with this.

As Chloe and many others expressed, maternity leave is viewed as standard—a right that is routinely given to all employees. In contrast, while most academic women I interviewed did receive some form of maternity leave (most often under FMLA), nearly all discussed having had some concern over whether or how that leave (and, in particular, how *paid* leave) could be claimed.

In the military, rank is less associated with increased benefits and more with increased authority. Service members are required to follow a very strict chain of command, whereby they are required to deal almost exclusively with their immediate supervisor, and only in very exceptional circumstances is that chain of command to be superseded. An individual who breaks the chain of command inappropriately is potentially subject to consequences as significant as demotion, discharge, or even imprisonment. The chain of command is so embedded an aspect of the military as an institution that none of the interview participants had broken it, nor did they mention anyone else who had broken it. By threatening to "go congressional" during her time overseas, when she was not able to express and store her breast milk, Chloe came the closest to breaching the significance of the chain of command. As a consequence for simply threatening to disrupt the formal structure of rank in her institution, she was withheld a decoration at the end of her overseas tour.

An important question that Chloe's experience raises is why servicewomen describe having difficulty claiming their rights to breast-feeding, or other types of work/life balance policies, when they do not seem to have this trouble claiming basic convalescent leave. These policies seem to apply just as universally as maternity leave policies across ranks in the military. What explains the difficulties that some women described? While "appropriateness" within ranks is codified in some way in both institutions, much of what is deemed appropriate or inappropriate within the hierarchical structures of academia and the military is also *informal*, and normatively driven by other actors within the institution. These actors, and their understanding of appropriateness, also drive most of the institutional constraints concerning rank that the interview participants described experiencing. As Vicky, an associate professor and mother of two who has been at Elm University for over eleven years, says, "I mean, when it comes to what you will claim, I think the further along you are and the more confident you are in your career, then you're more likely to ask for what you need, which is unfortunate, because the people who generally need these resources are not in that position." Just as Vicky describes women in lower ranks in academia as lacking "confidence" to claim their rights, Jane, a twenty-nine-year-old captain in the Marines, says that lower-ranking service members are also reluctant to claim their rights to institutional policies: "While there's a Marine Corps order that says you have to be given a certain amount of time and a space to do it, most women, you know, lower-ranking females, are not going to push that."

These feelings of constraint are not formal constraints, such as the chain of command or variations in policies according to rank. The constraints are institutional, driven by informal norms that exist in the institution, but they are also the result of a kind of institutional learning that these women have undergone. They have learned that certain norms of behavior exist within the institution and that some individuals within the institution are likely to promote adherence to these norms. If individuals who are interested in promoting adherence to norms are also in positions of power relative to women who are interested in rights claiming or gaining knowledge about their rights, then they are able to maintain those norms through the use of formal or informal consequences. Rank therefore becomes salient not simply as an institutional structure where certain codified rights to benefits or processes of grievance are formally organized. Rank is also an informal structure within an institution, where individuals take part in maintaining its salience as well as the salience of other institutional norms through discourse.

Kay's experience illustrates this process concretely. In academia, the hierarchical structure is very much tied to the process of tenure. On the tenure track, Kay has formal expectations of a certain number of publications, service, and teaching, which are written into the rules that govern her institution. However, Kay also describes an awareness of expectations for tenure-track faculty that go beyond these formal rules. Kay has chosen to wait to become pregnant until after achieving tenure, because she perceives that those who would review her tenure case would expect her to achieve more than colleagues who had not had children. Even though Elm University has a policy where Kay would be entitled to stop the clock toward tenure, she has observed that, informally, individuals expect more. Furthermore, Kay fears consequences to her tenure review by these more senior individuals should she choose to mobilize her right to the stop-the-clock policy.

The significance of maintaining informal norms also begins to explain the discrepancies between the implementation of the military's maternity leave policy and the implementation of other work/life balance policies such as those for breast-feeding mothers like Chloe. Although regulations are very specific regarding the needs of pregnant and postpartum service members, their inclusion in the military is a relatively new phenomenon, and these regulations are very different from a blanket understanding of the need for "convalescent leave." This is a term that is stretched to meet the needs of postpartum women and does not recognize maternity leave specifically. Convalescent leave is a longer-standing formal policy, and it is not tied specifically to gender in the way that breast-feeding accommodations are.

Breast-feeding and other pre- and postpartum accommodations for servicewomen are more recent additions to regulations in all branches, and confusion around these policies abounds. Many of the servicewomen interviewed described feeling as though their superiors were unclear about the regulations that pertained to pregnant and postpartum women. An informal norm within their workplace therefore is that service members should not have to require special treatment beyond the scope of their usual duties. This norm seems to lead to some supervisors being unknowledgeable about policies that allow pregnant and postpartum women to modify their duties to accommodate physical needs. As Penny, a twenty-four-year-old former Navy seaman relates, "I know it is difficult for people that are at places where . . . the higher-ups don't know the rules; they don't know anything about what they're supposed to do for pregnant women."

Among the servicewomen interviewed for this study, several did not have the regulations properly applied to them. For each of these women, the chain of command became the default structure to which they submitted. Having had formal regulations applied improperly to their situations, these women were in the position of needing to push back against the formal and informal norms that structure rank within the U.S. military. Rank, for these women, was an extraordinary constraint on their ability to rights-claim. Yvonne's story is an excellent example of this. Yvonne is now thirty-three, but was a single mother in her mid-twenties when she served as a corporal in the Marine Corps and had her first child. She returned to work seven weeks after a cesarean and was incorrectly put back on full duty and would be required to participate in a three-mile squadron run immediately upon her return. In all service branches at the time of these interviews, postpartum women were in fact given four to six months after giving birth to return to their regular physical training requirements. When Yvonne mentioned this to her supervisor, his response was, "There's nothing I can do, you know; you have to go, and we can't get you back into medical." Yvonne notes that "he probably could've just ordered me not to go." But, she says, "when the order comes from above, he's like, 'You just have to show up and talk to the corpsman.'" Rather than straightening the mistake out himself, Yvonne's supervisor instead required her to turn up at the exercise, where she felt obligated to run. "I made it all three miles and I hurt so bad," she says. Eventually it became apparent during her run that something was wrong. Yvonne says,

I fell out at one point in the formation and somebody comes and starts yelling at me. I'm like "Listen, I had a C-section six, seven weeks ago" . . . and he just looks at me and he's like, "Oh, let's get the corpsman over here," and the corpsman came over and I'm like, "I feel fine if I just kind of jog/walk, I'll be—I think I'll be fine." I was in really good shape beforehand and during my pregnancy and so, she's like, "Yeah, just come see me afterwards; I'll just make it up right . . . you're going to have your six months."

And so she wrote it out for me. She's like, "That was wrong"; she's like, "But you know, it happens sometimes."

Yvonne did not feel comfortable confronting her supervisor about her right to reduced physical training requirements postpartum. Instead, she deferred to the appropriate action for her rank and position: she obeyed the order to turn up and run. Furthermore, the medical officer at the training exercise also knew that Yvonne had been denied her rights and was not surprised by her decision to adhere to the norms associated with her rank, nor did she question it. In fact, the Marine Corps written regulations permitted Yvonne to either question her supervisor or turn up for the exercise and insist on her medical status being changed then and there. Formal regulations therefore did not constrain Yvonne's decision making. However, informal norms around "appropriate" behavior within her rank *did* constrain her decision making. Yvonne deferred to her supervisor's decision to require her to run. In her case, the institutional constraints on her rights claiming were not formal or written, but based on her perception of the normative constraints of rank within the Marine Corps. Her position was not to question her supervisor but to obey his orders. Yvonne's story illustrates well the salience of rank as an institutional structure with both formal and normative rules and expectations attached to it.

Assigning particular policies according to rank, or requiring adherence to chain of command within formal institutional rules is one way of constraining women's rights claiming and decision making. But the informal action and interpretation of what is appropriate in a position in the hierarchy is also a way of maintaining the institutional structure of rank. Individual agency, and individuals' actions that work to create and perpetuate institutional rules and norms, are key to understanding how institutions act to constrain individuals in their formation of rights consciousness and their mobilization of rights.

Institutions as Enablers

According to a theory of discursive institutionalism, institutions do not simply constrain individual actors to maintain the status quo. They can also enable individuals to work for or effect change within the institution. The same formal and informal structures that constrain some members of an institution may be appropriated for the purposes of challenging norms or rules and effecting change. Institutional hierarchy or rank is once again a useful structure in which to critically analyze this process at work.

Effecting formal rule changes within an institutional setting can be difficult to achieve. As Valerie discovered at Elm University, often those who are most interested in change are those with the least power within the institutional hierarchy. Additionally, organizing collective action to initiate formal change, while not impossible (Oak University, after all, negotiated paid family leave through its faculty union in recent years), is often challenging. Effective collective action requires substantial resources and a shift in cultural expectations—or ideas—within the institution that makes the status quo no longer justifiable for a large number of individuals.[11]

But what part do individuals play in institutional change? Individuals may, of course, take part in or lead a collective effort. Carol, for instance, was part of a small team of women who worked to bring about the modification-of-duties policy at Elm University. However, collective action is not an individual's only potential for effecting change within an institution. Ideas are important in determining the policy agenda of collective movements that seek to challenge the status quo. It is therefore as instigators in the introduction, discussion, and perpetuation of ideas that individuals play a key role in institutional change. Institutions may indeed constrain the development of individuals' rights consciousness or their ability to rights-claim. However, institutional structures can also be appropriated to vocalize ideas that challenge institutional constraints and assert rights, particularly with regard to informal constraints.

Both faculty members and servicewomen interviewed for this study were enabled by institutional structures to challenge existing institutional norms. Within the academic case, for instance, some women described using their tenured status as a way to assert their rights openly. An excellent example of this is Carol, a thirty-nine-year-old tenured professor at Elm, who discussed using her tenured status to her advantage when she needed to breast-feed her baby while teaching—not an activity that Carol believes would have generally have been deemed appropriate at her institution:

I taught . . . a night class that was a class about violence. And I had to . . . breast-feed her. And I would do it in the hall sometimes, but occasionally I would, like, there she'd be, and I'd have a blanket over her, and I'd be gesticulating with one arm, talking about domestic violence and here's the baby breast-feeding. And I just remember being like, this is so freaky, you know. But it was sort of like—there wasn't the anxiety around that that I think would have been there had I been an untenured professor, because it kind of felt like, yup this is freaky, and they can't fire me, you know?

Similarly, Gina, a thirty-six-year-old mother of two who is an E-7 in the Coast Guard, says that she is using her rank as a way to challenge what she perceives is a norm among officers in the Coast Guard to not have more than two children:

I have never met, in the Coast Guard, an active-duty mom that had more than two kids. . . . I think it's a taboo, like, that everybody all of a sudden is gonna think wow, she's a baby machine now and, you know, kinda give up on me or whatever. . . . I have a promotion coming up this summer. I'll be making W-2 . . . so that was it, and I decided that I'm not gonna have the Coast Guard tell me how many kids I can have, I'm gonna do it.

Additionally, supervisors play a key role in the dissemination of ideas that affect women's rights consciousness and rights claiming. In many cases, women in both academia and the U.S. military described having their supervisors resist institutional norms on their behalf. Many others also described engaging in this resistance themselves on behalf of others. Pam, for instance, a forty-nine-year-old senior instructor at Elm, had her daughter before the modification-of-duties policy was introduced at her university. Pam says that if she had not been "able to spend as much time with my child as I really felt that I needed and wanted to do . . . I would have either quit my job or not had a child. . . . I definitely did not want to have to put my child in day care at six weeks." Pam did not have to put her child in day care at all, in fact, because her supervisor allowed her to take her baby to work with her every day for the first three years of her life. At work, Pam hired students to watch her child, taking her on walks around campus or playing with her in the office. This arrangement is certainly not typical at the university, but was not only supported by Pam's department chair; he was the one who suggested it to her. Pam explains that this kind of resistance to institutional norms by her chair is something that he does consciously and consistently. "My chair has always done stuff like the way he wants to do it and not exactly the way the policy is written or what's expected, because he decides what is right and does it. I mean he's very supportive of the faculty, and he's that way, really, for everyone."

Several servicewomen described similar experiences with their supervisors. Emma, for instance, a twenty-eight-year-old Marine, describes her supervisor as having "jumped through hoops" to accommodate her during her pregnancy and even visited her at the hospital after she gave birth in order to assist her to fill in her leave paperwork. Many other women acted or spoke up in resistance to institutional norms with which they disagreed, using their rank as a means of making this challenge effectively. Gina, for example, describes speaking up on behalf of lower-ranking colleagues if they are given a hard time about needing space or time to express breast milk.

In demonstrating that women have been able to use institutions to introduce and perpetuate ideas that resist the status quo, I do not mean to suggest that the enabling power of institutions is equal to their constraining power. To the contrary, there are far more examples in my interview data of women feeling constrained in their decision making by their institutional surroundings. Nine of the twenty-four women interviewed in the military are officers, and only five of the twenty-four women faculty interviewed are tenured. Indeed, the women who felt most comfortable trying to influence their institutional norms were all in positions of relatively greater power within their institution's hierarchy, and thus were less constrained by this institutional structure. However, this analysis demonstrates how ideas that are resistant to the status quo might be introduced into the discursive processes of an institution and might take hold. As one woman brings her child to class to breast-feed, another might see this action and interpret her institutional norms differently because of it. These are the roots of institutional change.

Conclusion

This chapter's empirical evidence supports a theory of discursive institutionalism. For the purposes of providing a consistent discussion of the discursive process at work, I focused primarily on rank, because both public universities and the U.S. military have a consistent ranking structure across specific workplaces that made this possible. Workplaces are discursive environments, and individual actors are constantly circulating ideas within them— ideas that both maintain and challenge the status quo. We have seen how women's rights consciousness and rights mobilization concerning work/life balance policies can be both constrained by formal and informal institutional structures such as rank and enabled by them.

Women from both case studies often described institutional hierarchy as something that affected either their ability to rights-claim (as was the case with Valerie) or their decision not to claim their rights (as in the case of Kay and Yvonne). Whether this constraint was due to formal rules associated with rank within the institution or, as was more often the case, with informal norms, institutional factors indeed proved to constrain women's rights consciousness and rights claiming.

Consistent with a theory of discursive institutions, however, the case studies demonstrate that women are able to employ the institutional structure of rank in order to introduce or perpetuate ideas that *resist* the status quo. This "enabling" aspect of institutions was specifically evident for women who had attained higher ranks within their institutions and were able to use this position of power to safeguard them against some of the consequences that women of lower ranks might suffer if they were to step outside the bounds of appropriate action for their rank.

In looking at the significance of formal and informal structures within this discursive process, this chapter demonstrates the important relationship between institutions and individuals—and the significance of ideas within that relationship. And yet it's worth considering which particularly salient ideas are affecting rights consciousness and rights claiming within the workplace.

5

In the Shadow of the Ideal Worker

Liv is a twenty-six-year-old Army sergeant in an airborne unit who, at the time of our interview, had an eight-month-old baby. When Liv found out about her pregnancy, her unit had just returned from a deployment. "There is no good or bad time to get pregnant in the Army," she says, but notes that "I was kind of in a good position because I did just get back from a deployment, so it's not like I looked like I was getting pregnant to get out of deployment." When asked whether this impression concerned her, Liv replied, "I mean, it's always in the back of your mind. . . . You know, my sergeant . . . one time, you know, I went to the motor pool to go and help and he goes, 'Ah, get out of here, you're useless,' . . . and I mean he was just joking, but he was also kind of like, you know, 'You can't do anything for me because you're pregnant,' so there is a stigma that's attached to it."

When Liv was transferred to a new unit early in her pregnancy, she had to confront the stigma head-on, since this new unit was due to deploy soon and was not the same unit with which she had recently returned from deployment. Liv says that she was so worried about how being pregnant would look in this situation that she offered to waive her postpartum period of deferred eligibility for deployment:

When I actually met the battalion commander . . . he said, "Oh, you getting ready to deploy with us?" and I said, "Well, sir, I'm pregnant, you know, and I'm due in February," and at that time, they weren't supposed to deploy until a little bit later, so I said, "I could waive my postpartum time and I can deploy with you guys," and he was all for that. He doesn't have any children.

Liv's immediate supervisor, a sergeant major, however, stopped her from doing this. "He said that he wouldn't allow me to waive my postpartum time to meet them in Afghanistan." Nevertheless, Liv's concern about how her pregnancy would look to her new lieutenant colonel and her fellow soldiers was concerning enough to her to consider relinquishing her right to defer deployment. The power of such stigmas around pregnancy and similar childbearing or child care needs extends to other service members and to women faculty in this study as well. These stigmas gain their power through their connection to the final thread of the theoretical framework for this book: ideology.

By examining the connection between institutional context and individual agency, we've seen how rights consciousness formation has developed around work/life balance policies for women in both military and academic settings. We've seen the role of individuals as agents in their own legal consciousness formation within a particular institutional setting and how formal and informal institutional structures act to both constrain and enable individuals to formulate, perpetuate, and pass along ideas. In this chapter, we examine ideology, looking both at how ideas about work/life balance rights are transmitted within institutional contexts and what ideas emerge as particularly salient.

One particular ideological construct that proved to be salient for all of the women in this study was that of the ideal worker. As we will see, this ideological construct pervades American workplace culture generally and was easy to spot in both public universities and the U.S. military. Exactly what the ideal worker looks like is highly institution specific, taking on unique institutional characteristics. However, it is possible to make strong connections across these institutional cases and see the general impact that this ideological construct has in helping to shape institutional stereotyping of working mothers. The relationship that I find between the ideological construct of the ideal worker and the development of public policy highlights the ways in which public policy can both combat and contribute to challenges that individuals face with rights claiming within an institutional setting.

The Connection between Policy and Ideology

Many sociolegal scholars before me have documented the significant role of cultural discourse in shaping rights consciousness and rights claiming.[1] Earlier in this book, we looked at the importance of informal norms to women's decisions about rights claiming in the area of work/life balance policies. It is clear that informal rules and norms can play a significant role in nullifying rights or in making the mobilization of those rights extremely difficult for individuals.

Informal institutional rules and norms are present in and shaped by larger cultural norms. As we have already seen, these institutional norms shape individual rights consciousness. Ideology is the thread that connects the individual, the institution, and the broader social consciousness. As discussed in the Introduction, ideology is a process of meaning making that reflects dominant strains of thinking. Such strains of thinking are present in the larger public discourse, filter into institutions, and are absorbed by individuals as they construct their rights consciousness. The decisions that individuals make about rights mobilization (or expressing their legal consciousness) then feeds back into the broader public discourse, either reinforcing hegemony or resisting it. The connection between ideology and rights consciousness is therefore not linear. Rather, legal consciousness shapes ideology, in that individuals are constantly involved in a larger discourse that serves to perpetuate or shift dominant ideologies over time. Therefore, ideology is, in a sense, time bound. It exists as something that is both constructing and being constructed in a particular historical moment. This time-bound nature of ideology is particularly significant in its relationship with public policy formation.

A large body of research indicates that policies themselves can be intimately connected to ideology, and the norms and informal schemas that exist within certain ideologies are present in the larger culture.[2] These scholars note that the relationship between policy and cultural norms may not simply be one of culture resisting policy but of culture *informing* policy formation. Ange-Marie Hancock, for instance, argues that a discourse of "disgust" around welfare recipients has led to the marginalization of recipients from the debate regarding welfare reform policy and the creation of policy that is informed by what is essentially an empirically debunked public image or stereotype.[3] Other scholars, such as Dorothy Roberts and Julia Jordan-Zachery, make convincing connections between the discourse surrounding Black women's sexuality and public policy formation.[4]

Not only does ideology shape legal consciousness and inform policy; policy choices that are historically embedded can also affect the formation of ideology and legal consciousness. Scholarship has indicated that policy backlash can give rise to stereotypes that may cause individuals even more difficulties with claiming their rights under policies aimed at improving gender imbalances.[5] This chapter lends support to these claims, indicating that social policy can have harmful effects on those it purports to help, particularly when its ideological implications are not taken into account. In the narratives that follow, it is clear that stereotypes exist around mothers in both public universities and the U.S. military. While these stereotypes are institution specific, they share one important characteristic: they reflect an institutional culture that stigmatizes mothers because they are taking time away from their work to meet family needs. The design of work/life balance policies to allow women to do just that has contributed to the creation and persistence of these stereotypes.

Ideology, Policy, and the "Ideal Worker"

Several scholars, most notably Joan Williams, have documented the existence of an ideal worker concept within workplace contexts.[6] Williams in particular has argued for its detrimental effects on women's decisions to seek out or take up maternity leave rights. In *Unbending Gender,* she argues that both men and women face challenges posed by the notion of the ideal worker, which she claims is pervasive in American workplace culture.[7] The ideal worker is childless or has an invisible caretaker at home, looking after domestic considerations and care needs so that the worker need not be concerned with these things. He or she is able to work full time and overtime, anytime. The ideal worker does not take maternity leave or need to pick up a sick child from school. The notion of the ideal worker, in other words, presents a dichotomy between "good" workers as those who are entirely devoted to their jobs and "bad" workers as those whose time and attention is consistently pulled to things outside work.

The ideal worker norm did not emerge from thin air. Rather, Williams argues, it is part of a larger ideology, which she calls an "ideology of domesticity." Williams documents how this ideology is both historically and still pervasive in American thought, culture, and law.[8] Susan Moller Okin is a feminist theorist who tackles the history of this ideology head-on, arguing that liberal theorists have long ignored women, relegating them to a "private" sphere that is irrelevant to the political or "public" sphere. It is the ideological separation of these two spheres that is the primary source of continued injustice for women, argues Okin.[9]

Yet the ideology and practice of domesticity remain intimately connected in American culture and politics. Several feminist scholars point to the significant connection between gender and caregiving expectations in the American workplace. Martha Albertson Fineman's work, for instance, emphasizes cultural ambivalence toward the strong caregiving ties of many women in the United States, arguing that it is this bond that should in fact be recognized by law and society as the nuclear family rather than the sexual bond of man and wife.[10] Laura T. Kessler follows in Fineman's footsteps and looks specifically at the traditional role of caregiver that a large percentage of women still carry out in their private spheres, arguing that law and legal tradition have systematically ignored this role and the impact of its existence on women's equality of opportunity in the workplace.[11] Kessler suggests that a normative solution is needed to adjust this disconnect, because it is the ideological undervaluing of women's caregiving work that causes it to be overlooked and underaddressed in the workplace.

Complicating this literature on the overlooked private lives of women is the growing body of scholarship critiquing the active role that many work/life policies have played in further entrenching gendered roles. Fathering literature, in particular, has highlighted this critique, illuminating the problematic emphasis in institutional policies and culture on the need for *women* to have time to care for private needs, while men are expected to maintain their public identities without giving attention to private ones. As the fathering literature demonstrates, men are not only increasingly interested in being more involved in the development and raising of their children;[12] they can also make distinct and important contributions to child rearing.[13] Other studies have demonstrated the challenges that specific public policies and institutions pose to rectifying the imbalance of caretaking due to their contribution to perpetuating gendered identities.[14]

The policies that have resulted from this historical and contemporary connection between women and caregiving roles, therefore, have emphasized the need to give *women* time away from work to care-give. This ideological connection is so strong that even when men are granted equal leave time for caregiving, women are still much more likely to take the time than men. According to the Bureau of Labor Statistics, women were thirty times more likely (3.2 percent of women taking leave, compared with .01 percent of men taking leave) to cite birth or adoption of a child as their reason for taking leave in any given week in 2011, even though they were only 3 percent more likely than men to take leave from work overall.[15]

This continued connection between the ideology of domesticity and public policy has unforeseen consequences for women's equality. Let us turn to the interview data to discuss ways in which the ideologies of domesticity—and the ideal worker norm—have had a significant impact on the rights consciousness and rights claiming of women in both public universities and the U.S. military. Women who participated in this study identified two distinct workplace stereotypes tied to the ideal worker norm, and we will see the ways in which these women wrestled with the stereotypes when thinking through their rights.

Mothers Are Not Ideal Workers

Literature on both academia and the U.S. military documents to some extent what is expected of an ideal worker in these environments. In academia, for instance, faculty are expected to pursue tenure-track careers that lead to full professorship, which most often requires a grueling research and teaching schedule. These expectations are frequently coupled with an understanding that faculty must not have commitments that take their time and attention away from these expectations, particularly the research element. Recent studies of male and female academics, for instance, have demonstrated that the individuals in these careers who are most successful at maintaining a high level of research output are married men with children and the least successful are married women with children.[16] These findings further emphasize the significance of unpaid domestic work in the ideal worker construct. Married men with children are successful, the authors of these studies suggest, because a female partner either fully or largely completes the "second shift" of housework and child care within the home, allowing them to devote more time to their primary career. Married women with children are, conversely, doing a disproportionate share of the domestic work and are thus disadvantaged in the time they are able to devote to paid work.[17]

In the military, the ideal worker is much more overtly masculine. As Cynthia Enloe notes, masculinity and the U.S. military are intimately connected. The ideal worker in the U.S.

military is a "warrior"—specifically, one who is male.[18] Yet in a volunteer military, recruitment of women soon became necessary in order to sustain its numbers. In opening the military to women, Enloe argues, officials "believe that they need to recruit and deploy women in only those ways that will not subvert the fundamentally masculinized culture of the military."[19] A woman in the U.S. military, therefore, is not an ideal worker simply by virtue of being female. Pregnancy and childbirth complicate this by reminding a woman's colleagues and superiors of her femaleness in very explicit ways. In both the U.S. military and public universities, my interviews demonstrate that institutional stereotypes have developed around women with children in these workplace settings as individuals who do not—and cannot—meet the expectations for an ideal worker.

The Military Mother Who Is Avoiding Deployment

In my interviews with military servicewomen, it became clear very quickly that a stereotype existed, and each of the women I spoke to was in some way reacting to it. In all but one of the interviews, the service member identified the stereotype explicitly. Essentially the stereotype is that women who become pregnant in the military do so in order to avoid their duties as warriors in some way, though the duty most frequently referenced was overseas deployment. Mothers in the U.S. military therefore do not fit the ideal worker image in their workplace because the ideal worker in a military environment is one who is physically fit and always ready to do his or her duty when called on. A pregnant service member does not fit this model in that she receives "special treatment"— which includes deferral from deployment for four to twelve months after childbirth[20] and exemptions from other typical duty requirements, such as uniform regulations or physical training exercises.

In detailing what the stereotype is, many of the women I interviewed were also careful to identify themselves as individuals who do *not* fit the stereotype. Grace, a thirty-three-year-old sergeant first class in the Army, clarified that she was aware of the stereotype but that she wasn't deployable when she got pregnant:

I mean there's a little bit of a stigma for people—especially women—that are staying behind [from a deployment]. . . . It's "Oh, did she get pregnant to get out of deployment?" I mean—which, I'd been pregnant before it was even known that we were deploying, but there's still always that little bit that, you know, the possibility of that chatter . . . it's more—I think, more of a gossip thing."

Grace goes on, however, to point out that she knows another woman who might better fit the stereotype:

[A soldier under my supervision] was actually in Afghanistan when she found out she was pregnant. . . . From the view of the command, they were not out to do her any favors. You know, she got sent home; technically she could have been punished. I mean, it didn't happen, but it definitely leaves a bad taste in the command's mouth in a situation like that.

Similarly, Joyce, fifty-eight, currently serves as a colonel in the Air Force. As a captain, she left active duty for the reserves when she decided to start her family and reentered only when her children were school age. "I separated [from active duty] what, a year and a half before the war [in Afghanistan] kicked off, so it wasn't like I did it because I had to go to war," she explains, clearly indicating her knowledge of the stereotype and her own position outside its reach. She continues, though, to relate that

a friend of mine was in a similar situation only she delivered her baby in August of 1990 . . . and her husband was already deployed to Desert Shield, and when she came back to our squadron, which is a deployable squadron, a flying squadron, she went over to a nondeployable squadron . . . and people talked about that. Even years later people talked about that, how she was given special treatment or that she didn't do what she should have done, which was deploy.

Sophia, a twenty-three-year-old third-class petty officer in the Navy, had a harder time defending her position in relation to the stereotype. Sophia, who is not married, became pregnant unintentionally while on a deployable ship and had to leave her boat for shore duty as a result. She insists that she is not one of the "girls who mess up" and "put a stigma on all the rest of the pregnant girls." Yet she felt as though she needed to hide her pregnancy from her fellow sailors when she left her ship, fearing that they would think she fit that stereotype:

There were a few people like that, they were like, ah, yeah, I see what you're doing, you know. And I kind of tried to keep it really quiet that I was pregnant when I was leaving. I told a lot of people I was leaving because of a bad back. So I didn't want to be known as that girl who got pregnant or got knocked up and had to leave the boat.

Many of the servicewomen who were interviewed also went beyond simply mentioning the stereotype and defining themselves in opposition to it. A number of them also said that their decision making, or that of other women they knew, has been influenced in whole or in part by the existence of this stereotype. For instance, some, like Gina, a chief petty officer in the Coast Guard, said that they consciously tried to work harder than their colleagues as a way of combating the image. Gina says:

I feel like already because we're females we have to work twice as hard to earn the respect that the males are already given, and then when you have these impressions running around in everybody's minds, and then it just—it spurs me on even more. I moved up pretty quick in my advancement, and a lot of that is just my initiative and my drive to prove people wrong. I'm tired of hearing it.

Adrienne, a thirty-eight-year-old Air Force major, took a similar though slightly different approach to combating the stereotype. During her pregnancy, Adrienne took pride in doing tasks that were above and beyond those recommended by her military profile.[21] She talks about meeting wounded warriors on the flight line right up until delivery, and also braving a massive snowstorm to go into work at eight months pregnant because she knew she would be able to get there before her supervisor to make sure that her work was being overseen at a critical time. She says she made these decisions because "I just didn't want them to appear that I was using my profile to get out of work"—and that she was "just doing what you're supposed to do as a leader." She says of her profile:

I think it recommended like you not stand for so many—for such a period of time or something like that—and then it allows you to wear tennis shoes if you wanted. Which is another thing: I never wore tennis shoes. I was so proud not to wear tennis shoes my whole entire pregnancy. I wore my boots—my combat boots—the entire pregnancy. I guess I just didn't want them to think that because I was on profile, I was taking the easy way out.

Adrienne takes pride in wearing her combat boots while pregnant and performing other tasks that she would be within her rights under military regulation to forgo. In this way, she is signaling to herself and to others that she is an ideal worker. She does not fit the stereotype but rather is eager to show others that she does not need to claim her rights as a pregnant member of the Air Force. Adrienne's behavior reflects a consciousness that rights claiming would make her stand out as nonideal. As we saw in the opening vignette, Liv too was quick to adopt behavior that would help her to stand out as an ideal worker in her new unit, stating her willingness to deploy earlier than required postpartum. For both Liv and Adrienne, waiving their rights to work/life balance policies aimed at improving their conditions in fact became a way for them to mark themselves as ideal workers.

Not all of the servicewomen felt that their decision making due to the stereotype was a way to combat it. Some of them said that they knew that a lot of their colleagues simply accepted that children and the military do not go together. Gabrielle, a thirty-six-year-old lieutenant colonel in the Air Force says, "A good number of us [mothers in the Air Force] will punch[22] [leave the military altogether] at that ten-year point. Because at that point in time, you've either gotten married or you haven't and you want to, and you've had children and you're trying to balance and it just—something's gotta give basically." Women who leave the military after ten years of service lose out on significant benefits and compensation that can be attained only after twenty years of service. The existence of the stereotype, Gabrielle believes, causes many women to think that balancing a military career and family is simply not possible and so they leave, meaning that women are much scarcer in the higher ranks, where length of service is a prerequisite. This trend in the military is strikingly similar to the problem of the leaky pipeline in academia, where women are also largely underrepresented at the higher ranks.[23]

While not all of the servicewomen interviewed felt that they had been especially harmed by the existence of the stereotype, a few did. Zoe, for instance, the Air Force veteran whose story was told in Chapter 2, had felt specifically targeted by her supervisor for retaliation because of her pregnancy. Even when more formal consequences are not evident, some of the women claim that the effect that the stereotype can have on relationships, with both their chain of command, and their colleagues, can also be significant. Brianna, a thirty-four-year-old Army specialist with two children, whose husband is also serving in the Army, felt personally targeted because of the existence of the stereotype about mothers in the military. She says that not long after having her first child, she was deployed to Kuwait. "Little did I know, I was pregnant with my daughter. . . . [My] first sergeant was irate. She was livid. She told me I should be a housewife. That the Army isn't for me. I'm a substandard soldier. She gave me forty-five minutes of what she thought about me being pregnant." Brianna said that she felt particularly hurt by being a target of this first sergeant, because prior to this incident, she had looked to her as a mentor for how to become a strong female leader in the military. "She really got in my head, she really messed with me. . . . I joined the military to serve my country. I come from kind of like a rich background of military in my family. And so for me to deploy, I was very proud. . . . So a lot of me felt like I let my unit down, I let myself down, I let my family down." Their relationship remained strained, and Brianna was relieved when she was later transferred and no longer required to work with that supervisor.

The Academic Mother Who Is Not a Serious Scholar

Women faculty working in public universities identified a stereotype with features unique to academia but nonetheless strikingly similar to that faced by U.S. military servicewomen. Most of the women interviewed referred to an explicit stereotype:

that women who have children at an academic institution are not serious scholars. In addition, the minority of these women who did not explicitly reference a stereotype still talked about how having a family could cause them professional difficulties, but their discussion of this tension was more implicit.

Some of the women faculty referred to interactions with colleagues in their workplaces where the stereotype and how to counteract it were discussed outright. Valerie, for instance, a visiting assistant professor with a two-year-old son, discusses how this stereotype was related in stark terms to her by another female colleague:

It was like Labor Day or something, that we had classes, but none of the local public schools had classes. A couple of the parents brought their kids to the office. But I did have someone tell me—I didn't bring my son—but I did have someone tell me, you know, "As a woman I wouldn't do that if I were you. People have trouble taking moms seriously, and they won't take you seriously if they see you walking around with your son. They won't think you take the job seriously."

Carol, a thirty-nine-year-old associate professor with a young child, says that she also had an interaction with a colleague that made her aware of the stereotype.

[My colleague] is a woman who is not—does not have a partner and does not have kids, and . . . she is a person who—the excessive energy around— "Oh let's talk about your kids, oh it's so exciting that you're pregnant"—felt suspicious to me. . . . I mean, it was very nice of her . . . but I just remember feeling like she was wanting to peg me as, okay, now she's a mom. Like, she's not really a scholar, she's a mom, and so I'm gonna talk to her in a baby voice about the kids. . . . I don't think that this was intentional. I don't think that this was, you know, some sort of consciously hostile thing. But it felt to me like I'm being stereotyped.

Overall, the women employed at the public universities seemed less concerned than the servicewomen had about needing to distinguish their own position outside the stereotype. Though some women, like Carol, indicated that they have made conscious choices to avoid being stereotyped, not every individual interviewed made this distinction as starkly or as comprehensively as the servicewomen did. Furthermore, none of the female faculty felt a need to point out that while she did not fit the stereotype, other female faculty did. Instead, the faculty who identified the stereotype explicitly went on to deny its validity.

Nonetheless, each woman interviewed discussed the difficulties that she had faced in trying to do her job well while balancing it with her family demands. Therefore, the phrase *work/life balance* (and a concern for achieving it) was a consistent theme across these interviews. What seemed to be a trend among academic women was to discuss the choices that they had made in response to these demands. Many of the female faculty interviewed said that their knowledge of the stereotype had caused them to feel conflicted or anxious about navigating work/life balance policies. Additionally, some faculty admitted that a consciousness of the stereotype had some serious effects on their decision making. Therefore, while female faculty members, on the whole, were not as willing to openly acknowledge that the stereotype correctly characterized some women in their profession as the servicewomen were, they nevertheless struggled to define themselves in opposition to it, indicating its significant impact on their rights consciousness.

Several of the academic women, like the servicewomen, talked about feeling the need to work harder to counter the narrative that they are somehow shirking their duties. Louise, for example, an assistant professor at Oak University with four children, says that she feels anxiety about appearing to be a good worker. "I mean . . . I don't want people think that I'm just cashing it in—taking advantage of people's goodwill." Louise talks about feeling guilty for not making her time on bed rest with her latest pregnancy count more in terms of working toward her publishing record. "I mean, I read tons of stuff online, you know . . . like, everybody dreams of having seven weeks where you're sitting on your bed doing nothing but that . . . but it doesn't ever work out that way." Louise goes on to say that even though she worked on article revisions and read during this time, and despite being "on track" with her publication record, she felt that "I lost that summer." Vicky, too, an associate professor whose story is told in Chapter 1, had admitted to working while on maternity leave for similar reasons. These stories are consistent with a recent national study of U.S. mothers, which reported that 43 percent of women surveyed did at least some work for their employer while on maternity leave.[24]

Other academic mothers felt that they had to make some difficult personal choices in order to respond to the stereotype. Constance's story, for instance, provides a clear example of engaging in personal sacrifice to conform to ideal worker norms. Terrified of becoming pregnant at the "wrong" time in her career, Constance chose to undergo physically demanding hormone therapy in order to conceive within a certain window of time. Marie, too, made a personal choice that for her was extremely difficult. Marie is a thirty-one-year-old visiting assistant professor who does not yet have children and is waiting to do so until she secures a tenure-track job. She feels that the stereotype is particularly acute for her as a visiting assistant professor. Although she wants to ask about policies available to her, she says, "It's this question you're told you cannot ask because it'll work against you in the job evaluation, and they'll assume that you're about to go out and have a whole litter of babies, so—yeah, I feel very silenced about [it]. I couldn't ask if just in case, what are my rights, how would you handle it—nothing." In addition to this tension, Marie also feels conflicted because she is a Catholic and until recently was not using birth control. As a married woman, Marie faced a potentially impossible situation: "The choice I was looking at was not so much contracept as not contracept, although that was my solution. The choice I was looking at is abortion or my career . . . that's not a choice."[25] Marie made a difficult decision for her to go against the teachings of her religion and use birth control in order to counteract the stereotype that she faces in her career.

Most commonly, however, the academic women who were in faculty roles mentioned making career sacrifices in order to be able to better balance the demands of their jobs and the demands of their families. This decision seems to be a way of trying to take ownership of the stereotype and nullify its significance by discussing it in terms of personal choice. Alex, for instance, says:

Yeah, I think at some point I decided, am I going to be the most aggressive publisher in the world, or am I going to be okay with not being the most aggressive publisher in the world, and spend more time with my kids? And I made that decision, and, you know, I was a little worried. I did fine with tenure—I was a little worried with tenure, I think everybody is—but I certainly at that point, when I was turning in my packet,[26] I was like, I wish I had been a little bit more productive at least, you know, somewhere in there. But at the same time, it was a decision I made.

Alex takes responsibility for her decision to make some career sacrifices to attain a better work/life balance. At the same time, the stereotype of her as someone who is not as serious about her career seems to have caused her some doubt about her choices when she was going up for tenure. Therefore, although her personal decision making was a way of voicing her autonomy from the stereotype, she was not entirely able to escape its power to cause her anxiety.

As was the case with the servicewomen, not all of the women faculty members interviewed said that they had felt personally targeted because of the stereotype. A few, however, did witness or experience personal attacks or discrimination because of their decision to have children. One assistant professor interviewed, who does not yet have children but is thinking about having them in the near future, was not affected herself, but she had a friend who she felt had been targeted, and this experience made her wary of having children before tenure:

One of my colleagues went up for tenure, and she had stopped the clock, and she was just really, really worried about tenure, because—she ended up getting it, but I guess at her panel interview, what she told me was that people had said like, "You know, you had that whole extra year. What were you doing?" And she said, "Well, you know, I had an infant at home. I wasn't really—I just didn't have the opportunity to focus on my research. It wasn't like a sabbatical year," and just even having to defend that just seems really shortsighted to me.

Other women felt more directly targeted. Danielle, a thirty-two-year-old visiting assistant professor with a young child, says that she felt singled out by a fellow faculty member while pregnant. Her job involves fieldwork, so she was frequently out in the field working rather than in her office. "I had a particular faculty member contact the dean telling the dean that I'm not in my office, that I'm not doing my job, because I'm not face-to-face. And so I got an e-mail that was forwarded from my dean, asking where am I, and I simply replied, 'I'm in the field.'" Danielle expressed, like many of the other women interviewed, that she had been working extra hard during her pregnancy to make up for the fact that she was going to take time off. That was why this colleague's behavior seemed especially perplexing to her. When asked why she thought that colleague had targeted her to report to her dean, Danielle, who also identifies as African American, said, "She was very, very conservative in her beliefs, and being at the time unmarried and pregnant, probably added to her personal views toward me." In Danielle's opinion, the institutional construct of the ideal worker reinforced and heightened other ideological constructs that this coworker held in her mind about who is a "good mother." Danielle thus found herself unable to meet the expectations of this colleague for *either* an ideal worker or an ideal mother.

Nora, a mother of two children, felt even more explicitly targeted because of the stereotype. Nora is an associate professor and administrator. When she was applying for an advanced administrative position a few years prior, Nora recounts that her interviewer said something surprising to her: "She said she was concerned about my ability to do the job because I had a child. . . . So at that point in time I was like . . . you've got to be kidding me." Nora was not chosen for the position. Nora says that she feels her job and the stereotype that exists in her place of work is counterproductive. "There's nothing enlightened about that." The first reaction when someone has or adopts a child, says Nora, "ought to be, 'Congratulations! How can we make it so that you can enjoy and have a healthy experience for you and your child, and then embrace you so that you come back to us ready to go,' and that's just never happened that I've seen."

Eve, a thirty-three-year-old mother of two who is an assistant professor, said that she almost didn't return to her job in the year that she was interviewed because of an experience where she had felt targeted as a mother at work. She said that at first, her supervisor and her colleagues had been excited and happy for her when she returned to work from maternity leave with her most recent child:

And then as we started to get into the evaluation process of my work, those conversations kind of started to change a little bit. Like my evaluation, my midtenure review. I started getting comments. I had my lowest annual review the year that I [took maternity leave], with the comment written that my personal life was affecting my work. . . . Comments being made perhaps I should consider getting a nanny instead of using child care if I wanted to be successful in my job. Have I ever thought about working part time, so that I can spend more time at home with my children? Comments like that from my colleagues and from my immediate supervisor that I was not expecting. . . . It made me start to think that maybe I couldn't do it. Like, wow—maybe I can't be the mom that I want to be and be the professional that I want to be at the same time, and it really kind of started to weigh heavily on me, reconsidering my options for employment. Maybe I needed to go part time; maybe I needed to do different things. I almost didn't come back this year.

Paradoxically, when asked whether she personally felt that her performance at her job had suffered because of having her second child, Eve emphatically denied it: "No. Not at all. Not at all. I felt like I was able to balance it. I had a great support system at home, and so I thought I . . . was doing fine. I really did. . . . I actually felt—hey I can do this! Like, this is really manageable. So I was really surprised with the outcome."

In both public universities and the U.S. military, each of the women interviewed had either an explicit or an implicit understanding of the ideal worker norm as it exists within her institution. The expectations of their individual jobs are drastically different, but the ideological construction of gender identities, which set expectations on women that they should be primary caregivers and in charge of the domestic sphere, leads to similar expectations of an ideal worker within each workplace setting. Ideal workers are not meant to be focused on what is going on at home, and women in these workplace settings are constantly struggling with that expectation. These women are also often doing battle in their workplaces with stereotypes that expect them to underperform in their jobs because they have domestic commitments. Although each woman in this study combats these constructs and the larger ideologies behind them differently, it is possible to see a clear connection between the ways that ideal workers are conceived within these institutions. Larger ideological constructs such as the ideal worker therefore permeate workplace cultures and take on unique institutional flavors. Yet the core of the construct remains and clearly affects how women think about and act on their rights in these cases.

The Role of Policy in Creating and Reinforcing Stereotypes

Most sociolegal scholarship has treated stereotypes as norms that operate in the "shadow of the law," governing attitudes and behavior in ways that are not governed by the law or are norms that perhaps have grown out of an absence of law. Norms that exist in the shadow of the law may even be in conflict with laws or policies themselves. Catherine Albiston discusses the power of such stereotypes to regulate women's abilities to bargain for their rights under the Family and Medical Leave Act. She notes that

over time, the interconnected and mutually reinforcing systems of meaning among gender, disability, and work have come to form an invisible cognitive framework that gives meaning to leave for family or medical purposes. In particular, seemingly neutral features of work, such as attendance and time invested in work rather than productivity, have come to define "good workers."[27]

The narratives presented here illustrate the relevance of Albiston's observation in broader context. The power of normative constructs such as the ideal worker (and the stereotypes that emerge around them) goes beyond what is possible to regulate with policy. Attitudes and behaviors such as those described in this chapter may be discouraged by the policies in place in these institutions, but hearts and minds cannot be effectively changed by policies alone, and in fact cultural change must often happen before policies can be truly effective. Indeed, this is one of the fundamental points made by the critical legal studies movement: "Liberal rights rhetoric ordinarily fails to consider that fundamental social changes are necessary to allow people to exercise their rights."[28]

While this observation alone is interesting and important, another significant finding emerges from this research. The opportunity for institutional comparison provided by these interviews—the ability to look at two very different workplaces, with very different policies and nonpolicy normative ordering— reveals connections that go beyond institution-specific norms. The stereotypes that are visible in the military and academia are all connected to values associated with being an ideal worker (with what is "ideal" having specific institutional characteristics in each case). Furthermore, the stereotypes that are present in these institutions indicate that mothers are being defined as antithetical to the ideal worker. They are in fact workers who shirk their responsibilities.

What is even more unsettling about these findings is that they indicate a close connection between the existence of institutional stereotypes of mothers and the policies aimed at protecting mothers in the workplace. Policies such as maternity leave, breastfeeding accommodations and duty, or uniform modification all offer important contributions to the health and well-being of mother and child. Yet the fact is that maternity and other work/ family balance policies create a legal environment in which mothers *are* receiving exemptions from workplace duties that other workers are not entitled to. The stereotype in the military is that military mothers are trying to get out of deployment, an essential duty, potentially required of anyone at any time. While it may not be true that an individual is trying to avoid deployment, a pregnant woman or new mother does not deploy with her unit. Pregnancy or childbirth and the subsequent deployment deferral make mothers an exception to that duty, putting them in stark contrast to the ideal male warrior who is able to do his duty at any time. Likewise, in academia, faculty members must "publish or perish," and in many other ways are expected to demonstrate devotion to the job. Mothers are exempted from the expectations of their jobs in academia to have children, if only for a time, when they stop the tenure clock, or take six weeks or more of maternity leave that keeps them out of the office and exempts them from teaching and service requirements.

The stereotypes observed in this book are important to record and wrestle with, not simply because they hold power in and of themselves to shape attitudes and behaviors (often in negative ways) but they also reflect the inherent problems in the current structure of work/life policies themselves. Work/life policies may often be implemented without taking into account how an institutional culture might react, and begin to shape norms and attitudes around those policies. Indeed, through an examination of the ideological discourse in two workplace-specific cultures, it is evident that as long as workplace policies are structured to exempt mothers from work for family needs in ways that other workers are not permitted to be exempt (or do not ordinarily opt to be exempted), then mothers will continue to struggle against stereotypes that paint them as workers who are (intentionally or not) shirking their responsibilities.

The ideology of domesticity—and its pervasive ideal worker norm in the context of two specific institutions—is incredibly salient. The ideal worker norm operates within these institutional settings, taking on distinct institutional flavors that are either explicitly or implicitly referenced by all of the interview participants, indicating their internalization to some degree or another. Each participant reacted to these stereotypes in different ways, and rights-claiming was not uniformly affected by the internalization of these norms. However, what factors affect how these women gain legal knowledge about work/life balance policies in their workplaces becomes clearer. By understanding the pervasiveness of these norms, their origins, and how they are communicated within an institution and internalized by individuals, it becomes obvious that public policy, born within a particular historical and ideological context, can both assist with and complicate rights claiming.

Conclusion

This is a particularly difficult juncture at which to conclude this chapter. Women in my interviews often cited the existence of work/life balance policies such as maternity leave and other "special accommodations" as having been essential to helping them stay in their jobs. Louise, an associate professor at Oak University, put it this way: "I needed those policies . . . those policies saved my ass." Yet it is also clear from this analysis that the current state of work/life balance policies is inherently problematic. Such policies rely heavily on an ideology of domesticity that perpetuates norms of women's caregiving. The persistence of this ideology within institutional policy then reinforces that ideology within workplace norms and cultures, which also creates additional tensions for women to navigate if they want to claim these policies. This analysis begs a larger societal discussion about how policies might be better designed and implemented to take these ideological and structural complexities into account. The final chapter takes up this question in more detail, using suggestions and commentary from the interview participants themselves about how workplace policies might better grapple with these ideological effects on rights consciousness.

Conclusion: Can Mothers Ever Be Ideal Workers?

This book has traced the complex ways in which individuals come to form their rights consciousness. What are the instrumental, institutional, and ideological mechanisms that shape how people come to think about themselves as rights holders and affect the decisions they make about whether to claim their rights? Better understanding how rights consciousness is formed leads to a better understanding of the efficacy of public policy in achieving its stated goals. In the case of work/life balance policies such as maternity leave, the intended goal may be to attract and retain qualified female employees, support them in furthering their careers, and provide some sort of equal playing field with men within their career trajectories. Yet one need only look at recent public discourse around women and work to note that the promises of such policies are not being met.

The interviews presented in this book paint a complex picture of women's interaction with work/life balance laws and policies. These women's stories call into question whether work/life balance policies, as they currently exist, are indeed making the workplace more equal. Their stories illuminate the wide gap between the promise of balance and their lived experiences. Women interviewed simultaneously recognize the ways in which work/life balance policies both help and hinder workplace equality. Many of them perceive such policies as attempts to help them. At the same time, many also point to ways that these policies in their current forms are sometimes problematic for their career advancement, workplace equality, and retention.

By focusing on three separate factors that affect the formation of rights consciousness, I hope to shed light on some important insights about the relationship between the individual and the social in rights consciousness formation.

The Promise of Equality

Many feminist theorists have long scrutinized formal legal equality—a model of legal equality that has as its priority women's assimilation into male-dominated spheres. This emphasis, which was necessary for early feminists to use in order to achieve formal equal treatment under the law (such as the ability to join certain sectors of education or the workforce), was in fact limited in its ability to bring women actual equality in areas such as the domestic and care workload, pay equity, and other aspects of women's day-to-day lives that were outside the reach of the law.[1]

The argument for maternity leave sprang from a change in the feminist movement from one that called for formal legal equality of women to one that recognized the differences between women and men. Specifically, many feminists began focusing on the physical aspects of childbearing and instead emphasized equality of *opportunity*. Christine Littleton refers to this as a transition from "symmetrical" models of sexual equality to "asymmetrical" models.[2] Herma Hill Kay's arguments for maternity leave as a method of dealing with women's physical differences in childbearing are an example of this "asymmetrical" model:

During the temporary episode of a woman's pregnancy . . . she may become unable to utilize her abilities in the same way she had done prior to her reproductive conduct. Since a man's abilities are not similarly impaired as a result of his reproductive behavior, equality of opportunity implies that the woman should not be disadvantaged as a result of that sex-specific variation.[3]

Other feminist theorists take an even more radical approach, arguing that this focus on the public sphere is problematic, and that it is the undervaluing of *private* work, such as caregiving, that is the true source of inequality.[4] Arlie Hochschild's work in particular highlights the significant impact of the "leisure gap" and the additional effects of domestic work on women who work outside the home.[5]

While all of these theoretical approaches have value in tackling the problem of women's inequality in the workplace, this book demonstrates that simply achieving women's increased *presence* in the workplace remains an important goal. This is especially true in workplaces where women are still underrepresented, such as public universities or the U.S. military, particularly within the higher ranks of these institutions. Over and over again, women in this book emphasized the significance of having other women in their workplace to turn to for help, advice, and support. More to the point, having women in places of power made an important difference to several of the women in their ability to rights-claim. As the discussion in Chapter 4 highlighted, while rank can be a constraining institutional structure for many women, it can also enable resistance to pervasive norms within an institution. Women in higher ranks in the workplace who can breast-feed publicly at work without fear of reprisal, or speak up on behalf of lower-ranking colleagues when their peers invoke hurtful stereotypes, are key to helping other women claim their rights in more ways than one. These higher-ranking women can certainly advocate on behalf of their lower-ranking colleagues. However, even without this direct advocacy, such counternormative action can have an important effect on an institution. The presence of women in higher ranks enables a process whereby rights consciousness within institutional settings can *change*. If institutions are discursively constructed, then individual understandings of norms and of policies themselves and how they are to be implemented can be fundamentally affected by other individuals with institutional power taking it on themselves to affect that discourse. This book calls attention to several instances where women cited the normalizing effects of other women (and men) having "gone before them" in their workplaces—claiming work/life balance policies or challenging ideal worker norms—and claiming that these actions were instrumental to their own rights consciousness formation. Moreover, such an impact on their rights consciousness did not necessarily require direct advocacy by these higher-ranking individuals. At times, merely observing certain attitudes and behaviors that ran counter to hegemonic ideological constructs within the institution was enough to empower and enable those at lower ranks to do the same.

The reality is that women continue to be significantly underrepresented within the higher ranks of both public universities and the U.S. military. In academia as a whole, according to an American Association of University Professors report, women comprise 46 percent of all full-time faculty, yet make up only 28 percent of full professors and 36 percent of academic deans.[6] In their study of the impact of child rearing on academic careers, Mason et al. found that women are 21 percent less likely to get promoted than their male colleagues.[7] The story is even starker for women in uniform seeking to gain the highest ranks in their career path. Women in all branches of the military make up just under 17 percent of all officers and just 7 percent of all top positions (generals and admirals). In some branches, this contrast is more striking than others. In the Marine Corps, for instance, there is just one female general.[8] While the number of women in higher ranks in both of these institutions has improved in recent decades, this shortage of women in places of power has real consequences today for women's rights consciousness and rights claiming, as the stories contained in this book have shown.

As I discussed in Chapter 5, the promise of formal equality for women in higher ranks within the workforce is fundamentally limited by powerful ideologies that still dominate American discourse around work and family. Ideal worker norms overshadow women's legal consciousness about work/life balance policies in both public universities and the U.S. military. Women in both institutions are attuned not only to the notion of an ideal worker construct within their institutions, but also to stereotypes that paint mothers as unable to fit within those constructs. Faced with these stereotypes, mothers in this study often found it hard to be taken seriously in their careers, which some felt affected them professionally, particularly in their career advancement. Women "leaking" from career pipelines because of childbearing "choices" or constraints have been cited for the lack of women in advanced positions in many professions.[9] Yet few studies have investigated the harm caused by ideological constructs in and of themselves on these recruitment and retention statistics—and on mothers' career advancement as a whole.[10] While the purpose of this book is not to provide a systematic study of the effects of ideal worker–inspired stereotypes on women's career advancement, it does provide evidence on which to base such future investigation. In this book, individuals' rights consciousness and rights claiming are linked with conceptions of the ideal worker. Future scholarship is needed on whether this ideological construct might be linked with other facets of women's equality in the workplace.

The discussion of the ideal worker norm and its related stereotypes highlights the limitations of women's formal equality in an additional way. The presence of women in the higher ranks of these institutions, while clearly important, is not enough to combat the ideological constructs that negatively affect women's rights consciousness and rights claiming. In order for institutionally embedded ideological norms to change, women must also *actively challenge* these norms. If women in the higher ranks of a workplace also ascribe to ideological constructs such as the ideal worker norm—and many interviewees pointed to instances of their female superiors doing so—then their mere presence in these positions is not enough to change cultural expectations. Indeed, a female supervisor's adoption of such ideology may even fuel its cultural power further. If a woman is seen to be perpetuating stereotypes pertaining to other women, then the justifications for that stereotype receive a greater degree of gravity.[11] This argument is in tension with recent popular discourse, encouraging women to be more assertive in the workplace. Popular *Lean In* author and Facebook chief operating officer Sheryl Sandberg, for instance, points to a "leadership ambition gap" between men and women and encourages women to escape from feminine stereotypes and "aspire to lead."[12] Internalizing and perpetuating workplace norms that are distinctly masculine in order to "get ahead" may indeed gain some women, such as Sandberg, individual success. Yet if this continues on an individual basis, nothing changes systemically. Women must still conform to gendered expectations in the workplace. Certain neoliberal ideals about what makes someone "successful" continue to go unchallenged. A recent blog post by Ellen Leanse on Women 2.0 illustrates this point.[13] The author, a former Google executive, noted that women used language such as *just* to hedge their arguments, whereas men do not. Comparisons between men and women in terms of their language or behavior in the workplace abound in popular discourse around women and work. However, what these well-intentioned authors miss is that such comparisons only serve to reinforce and entrench the superiority of such "masculine" language and behavior rather than calling it into question.

The Limits of the Law

One of the most striking things I observed while writing this book was the extremely limited ability of work/life balance policies to bring about real institutional change. We have seen how stereotypes connected to cultural norms can be reinforced by policies aimed at combating those very same norms. A woman may indeed claim her right to take maternity leave, only to return from this leave to find herself the subject of professional stigma and informal reprisal. This is a problematic observation for policymakers and those interested in effecting social change regarding women and their roles in the workplace because it underscores the difficulty of taking ideology and institutional culture into account in public policymaking. Additionally, policies such as maternity leave, breast-feeding accommodations, and other work/life balance policies are cited by many women (including those in this study) as instrumental to their workplace retention. How, then, can work/life balance policymakers reconcile this tension between these policies' complex relationship with entrenched ideology and their intended positive effects on women's workplace equality?

Several of the participants in this study weighed in on this very question. Many of them made the same connections between the stereotypes that surrounded them as mothers in the workplace and the policies aimed at improving their work/life balance. For these women, it is the inherently gendered nature of work/life balance policy that is the root of the problem. Jane, a twenty-nine-year-old captain in the Marines, points out,

If you're a pregnant female marine, then you're, you know, everyone knows you're taking maternity leave, so you're going to be away from work. You made a personal choice that is going to take you away from your job for a certain amount of time, whereas for a male marine who has a pregnant spouse, it is a show of virility. That's kind of a conflict.

In searching for answers to this tension, a few of the interview participants asked: What if work/life balance policies were aimed at *both* men and women equally? Some women pointed to an increase in recent years in men's interest in child rearing, arguing that work/life balance policies aimed at women do not cause problems only for women by stereotyping them as nonideal workers. In fact, it is conceivable that such norms are even harder for men to overcome if they are interested in using work/life balance policies. At least for women, there is an institutional expectation that they will be nonideal workers. Men, however, in choosing to take these policies, are aware that they are actively choosing to be viewed negatively. Some of the women in this study also cited medical, emotional, or cultural needs that men have to be caregivers, arguing that they are similar to women's needs. "Our dads need their time with their infant children, says Danielle, a visiting assistant professor at Elm University. "Especially those critical first couple of months." Perhaps, then, as these women suggest, the problem with work/life balance policies—why they remain so tied to ideological constructions women and care work—is their lack of male inclusiveness.

Unpaid paternity leave is in fact available under the Family and Medical Leave Act. Additionally, at both public universities in this study, as well as in the U.S. military, options for men to take advantage of work/life balance policies do exist. For instance, in both Oak University and Elm University, men were eligible to stop their tenure clocks upon the birth or adoption of a child. At Oak University, men are equally eligible to claim the paid family leave policy, and at Elm, they are also eligible to modify their teaching duties in the semester following the birth or adoption of a child. In other words, at the academic institutions, men and women had few differences in terms of the work/life balance policies at their disposal.

In the U.S. military, the story is somewhat different. Since 2008, male service members in all branches of the U.S. Armed Forces have been eligible for ten days of paternity leave upon birth or adoption of a child.[14] Many of servicewomen who took part in this study were married to men who also serve, but most of these women had given birth prior to the introduction of paternity leave. A few, though, did mention that their children's fathers had been afforded the leave but had mixed feelings about it. Some women claimed that it was not enough time for men to have off, especially when considering that women had six weeks, whether for birth or adoption of a child. Others complained that it was not being implemented correctly. Natalie, for instance, a twenty-nine-year-old Air Force major, says that her husband could not get his leave straight after their youngest child's birth:

He didn't get to take it. It was, like, backdated to him. I think with men they'll be like, "You can get it, but you can't have it now." . . . We didn't get to use it when he was actually born. It was maybe a month later, and I don't know if that's the correct way or not, but at the time that's what we did. I mean it would be nice if it was, you know, the two weeks once the baby is born and then the dad can go help too.

Sophia, too, a twenty-three-year old E-4 who was not married to her baby's father, was frustrated because he was told he could not have paternity leave because they were not married. "They would not give it to him, because he's not married to me. The ship said he wasn't entitled, though the regulations—they do say that he can have paternity leave, whether he's married or not. But it's harder for a father who's not married to the mother to fight for paternity leave."

Clearly, then, men and women in the U.S. military are significantly distinguished by sex in terms of their rights to work/life balance policies. Unfortunately, however, the policy solution to real institutional change does not lie in fixing such policy discrepancies between the sexes. The data presented in this book are consistent with findings elsewhere in showing that the problem is not that men do not have access to work/life balance policies like paternity leave; it is that even when they do, they do not take it. Klerman, Daley, and Pozniak, for instance, find that women are 30 percent more likely than men to take leave under the FMLA.[15] This discrepancy, that men have leave available to them and are not taking it but women are, can exacerbate the stereotype that women are not ideal workers. The fact that maternity leave is so often conflated with disability—or sick leave—compounds this problem. When asked about *why* they thought family leave was important, most of the women who participated in this study brought up the temporary physical disability that childbirth causes as a justification for maternity leave policy. However, women who adopt children or men who wish to take advantage of family leave policies aimed at fathers are not able to justify their leave taking in these terms. This serves to doubly stigmatize fathers who choose to take leave and further entrench gendered expectations of leave taking.

A few of the women who participated in the interviews suggested that one solution to this problem might be to make work/life balance policies like family leave not just equally accessible but mandatory. The argument is that this might help to diminish the problems associated with men opting out of the leave and would also help to combat the image of mothers as choosing to shirk their workplace responsibilities while fathers do not. "It would be great if it was mandatory for both men and women so that it wouldn't affect . . . people by gender," says Mandy, a member of staff at Elm University and thirty-four-year-old mother of three.[16] Natalie, an Air Force major and mother of five, agrees: "I think, you know, if being the dad in the military, they don't have to decide to take their leave it's actually just given to them . . . kind of two free weeks and then they can help everyone adjust."

As a country, Sweden has attempted to create public policy that does just this. Sweden mandates that men take at least two months off during a child's formative years and provides eligibility for much more time should a father choose to use it.[17] The resulting statistics suggest that such culture-conscious policies— while falling far short of achieving total gender equality—are pushing Swedish society in the right direction. Eighty-five percent of Swedish men take paternity leave, and women's participation in the workforce is around 72 percent—compared with around 60 percent for women in the United States.[18]

Sweden's policies, while moving society in a positive direction, have not secured total workplace equality. For one thing, the mandatory time that Swedish men must take is still less than most women in Sweden take off for caregiving. Sweden grants 480 days of partially paid leave that can be devoted to child rearing, mandating that only 60 of those days are taken by fathers. Though up to 240 of these days *can* be taken by men, in reality, only about 12 percent of Swedish couples share this time equally.[19] Additionally, women's workforce participation in Sweden was still only 89 percent of men's in 2013.[20] The mandatory element of the policy may therefore solve some problems, such as men not being expected to take leave at all for child care, but it has not fully dealt with the unequal caregiving expectations of men and women, or equalized women's workforce participation. Additionally, Sweden's approach does not take into account the discrepancies that occur between men and women who have children and those who do not.

Another problem that mandatory leave does not fully address is the physicality of childbearing that women and men experience differently. Marie, a visiting assistant professor, who wants to have children but does not feel she can yet, explains why this may be:

I think part of it is because in many institutions, their policy about getting women into the academy is to assume that women are like men and treat them like men too. And there's something to be said for gender neutrality, but I think it also fails to address the fact that . . . anatomically . . .

pregnancy and childbirth create a blackout date that exists for women and not so for men, no matter how generous your leave policy is for new fathers.

Paternity leave, even at its most generous, has never fully addressed the connection between ideology and policy in the area of work/ life balance. Even in Sweden, where public policy has tried to engage cultural caregiving expectations in perhaps the most comprehensive way thus far, public policy has never fully eliminated the problem of the ideal worker norm. It is likely unrealistic to expect workplaces in the United States to adopt similarly generous work/life balance policies in the near future. Yet this recognition of the limitations of current work/life balance policies must not be confused with a critique of the initiative to bring about equality in the workplace for women through public policy. While policy is indeed limited in its ability to bring about social change, is it far from futile. The rights to maternity leave, to express breast milk at work, and in other ways to make balancing work and family life possible have improved the daily lives of many working women in America and have made staying in the workforce possible, as several women who participated in this study have attested. These rights represent an important step forward for women's equality, and formal, legal recognition that something must change about the historical exclusion of mothers from the workforce. As Patricia Williams points out, "rights" is the "magic wand of visibility and invisibility, of inclusion and exclusion, of power and no-power."[21] However problematic these policies may be for women, their existence represents recognition on the part of a company (or, in the case of FMLA, the country as a whole) that mothers are valued as employees too. Any suggestions for policy change therefore must take into account the lived experiences of the women the policies are meant to help and recognize both the harm and the good that these policies are doing in their current form. The policies themselves have been important tools for individual women in improving their personal circumstances, and this must not be undervalued. However, this book calls attention to the fact that public policy has been much less effective at bringing about *systemic* changes to the way that work and family are imagined and structured in American society. Furthermore, this failure is due not simply to their lack of generosity[22] but, more fundamental, to their continued connection to deeply entrenched ideology that surrounds caregiving in America. It is, in other words, only through changes in societal and institutional ideology that social change can be achieved. Public policy, in and of itself, is a poor tool for achieving social change.

Towards Solutions: Changing Workplace Discourse

The best way forward for work/life balance policy is to consider more closely that workplaces are discursive institutions, and the key to changing workplace culture lies in changing institutional discourse. There is an important caveat here, however. As we have seen, the ideal worker norm is not a workplace-specific ideological construct, but rather something that is much broader and more pervasive in the American psyche. I am not suggesting that a few simple policy fixes will bring down generations of ideological norms. I am, however, arguing that social change *starts* with changes in discourse. As we have seen, changes in institutional discourse can have a profound impact on legal consciousness and legal mobilization. Who is involved in the conversation about work and family is changing as the makeup of the workplace has gradually changed to include more women and mothers, and these individuals have the opportunity to effect social change by changing the discourse about the ideal worker. This is not an easy norm to tackle, as this book has shown. It is possible, though, for institutions to better support those individuals who challenge the idea that mothers are not good workers.

In *Making Rights Real*, Charles Epp documents the effects of court-led reform on bureaucratic practices, trying to understand how legal tools can play a part in helping activists to push forward social change.[23] He finds that practices such as programs to ensure strict implementation and compliances with policies—such as training programs, continued verbalized commitment to policies from administrators, and formal internal oversight—drastically improved the effectiveness of policies aimed at social change. The women interviewed in this study also discussed again and again how such measures aimed at improving policy *implementation* would help to negate the effects of the stereotypes they find themselves combatting. Much of the problem with institutional culture, argued some of the participants in this study, has to do with a lack of knowledge and understanding of the challenges that working mothers face in claiming their rights—whether these challenges are with formal policy claims or informal norms. The significance of educating the workforce about these policies, and their intended effects, was a recurring theme among the participants—particularly with women in the military.

Service members in all branches of the U.S. military receive a great deal of regular training. Gina, a chief petty officer in the Coast Guard, believes that these training requirements are a good place for the military to start changing the conversation about pregnancy and family in the services:

I think that when we are doing our annual required training and things along those lines that sensitivity as far as the issues of pregnancy in the workplace—being a working mom, and things along those lines—should be addressed. It should be similar to workplace harassment, or something along that lines. They should take a very strong stance.

The training alone is not enough, Gina argues; taking a "strong stance" is also important in order to demonstrate that the military is serious about changing its workplace culture. This argument demonstrates Gina's faith in the power of training to change institutional discourse, but only if the language of that training is forceful enough to convey that this is an issue the institution is serious about.

Once again, the significance of rank became salient when interview participants talked about the importance of combating the ideal worker norms with education in the workplace. Many women argued that individuals in leadership roles, who are aware of the problems that working women face, can be particularly effective. Emma, a twenty-eight-year-old corporal in the Marines, says that her experience with having her two-year-old was made significantly easier by the support she felt from her immediate supervisor, who was a father, and whose wife was pregnant at the same time as Emma.

I honestly think that a lot of how he was was because . . . he was a lot more sympathetic because he'd already been there. You know, as opposed to somebody who has never had kids before and really doesn't know what's going on with the mom or just with the pregnancy in general. I just think that really has a lot to do with it.

Brianna agrees that educating leadership in the military about the needs and rights of mothers would make a significant difference to how stigmatized they become. She thinks the military should "educate leaders more on what to expect. . . . Yes, we're girls . . . but we're not, you know, we're still soldiers. We're still out here doing the same exact thing. . . . Yes, we ovulate, and we do all that other stuff too, so you need to be prepared on how to deal with us. I don't think a lot of them are."

Educating institutional leadership as a means of combating ideal worker norms—and the stereotypes that are closely connected to them—takes into account the findings in all three analytical chapters of this book. First, it recognizes that changing the *conversation* in the workplace is crucial to more individuals claiming their rights to work/life balance policies and to those policies having their intended effects. Second, it recognizes the salience of rank within an institution and the power of higher-ranking individuals to affect institutional discourse disproportionately. Finally, it recognizes that leadership plays a key role in the institutional consciousness networks (ICNs) that individuals form in order to develop their own legal consciousness and to make decisions about rights claiming. Institutional leaders can provide important *informal* support to individuals within workplace environments, encouraging the good work that ICNs do in increasing rights consciousness and rights claiming, and playing an important role in challenging ideal worker norms.

The problem, of course, with proposing better education for institutional leaders in order to challenge ideal worker norms within their workplaces is that this proposal requires a genuine institutional commitment to changing these norms. The reality is that most workplaces are founded on capitalist goals, and the ideal worker is a construct that is fundamentally linked to capitalist ideology. This book focused on two institutions that are not ostensibly committed to capitalist ideology, since both the U.S. military and public universities have professed *public service*, rather than generating wealth, to be their central goal. The U.S. military prides itself on its contributions to public goods such as freedom, and its members are regularly thanked for their public service in all manner of public settings. Additionally, public universities are nonprofit organizations, committed to the delivery of public goods, such as teaching and research. Yet as the interviews have shown, employees of these venerable public institutions are not by any means immune to the capitalist ideology that infuses the ideal worker construct. While many institutions pay lip-service to ideals of equality and advancement for mothers (and parents) in the workplace, the reality is that most institutions and the individuals who lead them have a vested interest in perpetuating the ideal worker norms within their institutions, because these norms make workers produce—whatever the personal costs to individuals. In the past, what caused American workplaces to change their priorities when it came to things such as child labor, workplace safety, or overtime were not the workplaces themselves, but calls from society as a whole, or powerful segments of society such as unions, to improve working conditions.

In the previous chapters, we saw women networking with others in their workplaces in order to form their own rights consciousness and to rights-claim more effectively. These individual women are finding solutions to some of the issues with existing work/life balance policies through these social connections. The evidence presented in this book suggests that one possible avenue for public policy is to take these informal, institutional networks into account and find ways to support them. Institutional support for ICNs can take many forms. However, in supporting such networks, institutions must take into account the components that make these networks successful and be careful not to undermine what makes them useful. First, such networks are *institution specific*, so it is important for institutions to recognize and provide funds, space, and time for those groups that form internally. Second, ICNs are *independent* from institutions, so it is crucial that they remain free from institutional or administrative pressure. Finally, such groups are *informal* sources of information, support, and resistance, and their power lies in individuals using these networks instrumentally. Therefore, while institutions may help raise awareness for such networks, these networks should maintain a freedom from becoming institutional constructs in order to preserve their ability to resist institutional norms where necessary.

What might such institutional support for strategic consciousness networks look like in practice? In workplaces such as public universities, for instance, this might look like institutionally established faculty peer-mentoring groups. These groups can be entirely peer driven, with the only institutional input being funding, space, and time to meet regularly and independently from administrative oversight, in addition to raising awareness of the peer mentoring group's existence. In the U.S. military, this might look like well-advertised and funded support for breastfeeding support groups on each base. Crucially, such groups must maintain their independence from institutional pressure if they are to serve their critical functions in helping women to build their rights consciousness and to rights-claim. Institutional support, however, may be difficult to achieve without such pressure, and so achieving such support while maintaining institutional autonomy for informal networks will likely prove extremely challenging. In spite of these challenges, the support of ICNs may be the best hope for achieving real institutional and social change.

Can Women "Have It All"?

I opened this book with a question, often repeated in current public discourse: "Can women have it all"? The *promise* of work/life balance policies is inherently that a balance can indeed be achieved between work and life. Yet for each of the women interviewed in this study, that balance proved to be elusive, regardless of whether they chose to take advantage of the laws and policies available to them to help achieve such a balance. What these interviews demonstrate is not so much a problem with how the policies are constructed (although it has certainly revealed some big cracks that exist, such as the unequal application of such policies to all Americans). What has perhaps been more startlingly revealed is the way in which such laws and policies have largely failed to change the way that Americans fundamentally think about work and life. The problem, in other words, might not be that policies have not been designed properly to achieve work/life balance, but that Americans still imagine that such a balance *can* and *should* be sought. It is the promise of this elusive balance that is skewing the outcome. What Americans still seem to be unwilling to face is the reality that childbearing and child rearing are not things that can be balanced with work as though they are each on one end of a seesaw and one must simply adjust the weight on either end at times to make everything balance. Children and their care are necessarily messy and invasive things, and that will not change without the provisions that come with privilege, and even then the messiness of life never truly disappears.[24]

What *can* change is the other end of the seesaw. The ideal worker construct currently allows no room for the messiness of life to interfere or integrate well with work. However, unlike the reality of children, this reality is socially constructed. It is created and reinforced by ideology and can be changed. Right now, laws and policies are aimed at dealing with the "life" end of the seesaw—attempting to allow women to behave as ideal workers and keep family far away from work. An approach that may prove more effective at achieving true equity for mothers in the workplace is to construct laws and policies that challenge the hegemony of the ideal worker. For this task, I suggest that the support of institutional consciousness networks through policy may be a step in the right direction.

Institutional consciousness networks are where individuals are acting with agency every day to form their rights consciousness around work/life balance policies in their institutions. These networks are where individuals are turning in order to better navigate and challenge institutional norms and policies. Individuals who seek out others in order to shape their own rights consciousness and those of others around them hold the power to change institutional discourse and, by extension, public discourse. This is true for all women participating in these networks, and particularly for those in leadership positions. Public policy that creates rights for mothers in the workplace, recognizing them on paper as important citizens—even if that recognition is, at times, merely window dressing—is a significant step forward. But these rights are only one piece of the puzzle in improving the lived experiences of working mothers. The women in this study have sought ways to join together with other parents and supportive individuals in their workplaces to claim their rights and exercise resistance to ideal worker norms and the stereotypes that arise from them. Through these networks, the powerful image of the ideal worker can be effectively challenged and slowly chipped away. It is in this loose collection of individuals—the building blocks of collective resistance—that the real hope of social change lies for working mothers.

Appendix: Participant Information

Table 1   Respondents at Public Universities

Name	Age	Age of Children	Rank	Institution
Alex	35	Twins: 3 years	Assistant professor	Elm
Barbara	36	2 years; 4 months	Assistant professor	Elm
Carol	39	4 years	Associate professor	Elm
Charlotte	35	1 years	Assistant professor	Elm
Constance	39	3 months	Assistant professor	Elm
Courtney	43	None	Assistant professor	Oak
Danielle	32	4 years	Visiting assistant professor	Elm
Dolly	42	21 years; 18 years; 11 years; 3 years; 2 years	Associate professor	Oak
Eve	33	5 years; 1 year	Assistant professor	Elm
Kay	32	None	Assistant professor	Elm
Louise	37	6 years; 3 years; twins: 8 months	Assistant professor	Oak
Lyla	45	Twins: 1 year	Assistant professor	Oak
Lynn	32	2 years; 1 year	Assistant professor	Oak
Margaret	38	2 years	Adjunct professor	Elm
Marie	31	None	Visiting assistant professor	Elm
Nora	41	5 years; 2 years	Associate professor	Elm
Paige	49	9 years; 6 years	Assistant professor with tenure	Oak
Pam	49	6 years	Senior instructor	Elm
Pippa	38	5 years; 1 year	Assistant professor	Oak
Sally	41	5 years; 2 years	Adjunct/assistant professor	Elm

(continued on following page)

Table 1   Respondents at Public Universities (*continued*)

Name	Age	Age of Children	Rank	Institution
Taylor	38	1 year	Assistant professor	Oak
Tracey	38	3 years; 6 years	Assistant professor	Oak
Valerie	31	2 years	Visiting assistant professor	Elm
Vicky	NA	10 years; 6 years	Assistant professor	Elm

Note: All names are pseudonymous. "Age" refers to the respondent's and her children's ages at the time of interview. If a faculty member had children while working at her institution, "rank" indicates her rank at that time; otherwise, this indicates faculty member's rank at the time of interview.

Table 2   Respondents in the U.S. Military

Name	Age	Age of Children	Rank	Branch	Active Duty/ Reserve
Adrienne	38	18 years; 16 years; 15 years;2 years	O-4	Air Force	Active duty
Brianna	34	14 years; 2 years; 10 months	E-4	Army	Active duty
Chloe	37	Twins: 15 years; 4 years; pregnant	O-3	Air Force	Active duty
Daisy	50	6 years	O-5	National Guard	Reserves
Eileen	33	3 years; pregnant	E-5	Air Force	Active duty
Emma	28	2 years; pregnant with twins	E-4	Marines	Active duty
Gabrielle	36	10 years; 9 years	O-5	Air Force	Active duty
Gail	31	2 years; pregnant	O-3	Marines	Active duty
Gina	36	5 years; 1 years; pregnant	E-7	Coast Guard	Active duty
Grace	33	3 years; 1 year	E-7	Army	Active duty
Isabel	44	19 years; 14 years	O-4	Air Force	Reserves

Table 2   Respondents in the U.S. Military (*continued*)

Name	Age	Age of Children	Rank	Branch	Active Duty/ Reserve
Jane	29	9 years; 2 years	O-3	Marines	Active duty
Joyce	38	23 years; 20 years	O-3	Air Force	Reserves
Kelly	45	11 years; 10 years	E-6	Army	Active duty
Liv	26	8 months	E-5	Army	Active duty
Mackenzie	42	8 years; 6 years	E-8	Marines	Active duty
Natalie	39	21 years; 20 years; 15 years; 7 years; 4 years	O-4	Air Force	Active duty
Penny	24	2 years	Enlisted— unknown	Navy	Active duty
Piper	23	1 years	E-4	Army	Active duty
Quinn	38	17 years; 15 years; 10 years	E-8	Air Force	Active duty
Regina	52	24 years; 22 years	E-7	Marines	Active duty
Sophia	23	9 months	E-4	Navy	Active duty
Yvonne	33	12 years	E-4	Marines	Active duty
Zoe	29	7 years	E-4	Air Force	Active duty

Note: All names are pseudonymous. "Age" refers to the respondent's and her children's ages at the time of interview. If a service member had children while serving, "rank" indicates her rank at the time of having children. Otherwise, this indicates her rank at the time of the interview. Active Duty/Reserves" indicates the respondent's status at the time of the interview

Notes

Introduction

1. The *New York Times* ran a four-part series of essays authored by Adam Grant and Sheryl Sandberg entitled "Women at Work" between December 6, 2014, and March 5, 2015.

2. The episode of *Last Week Tonight* that aired on Mother's Day in 2015 (May 10, 2015) made the argument that celebrating mothers in America while simultaneously not providing for paid maternity leave is hypocritical.

3. Both the Trump and Clinton 2016 campaigns promised to introduce legislation that would implement paid family leave if elected.

4. Cohn et al. (2014).

5. Pew Research Center (2015).

6. Heilman and Chen (2005).

7. Williams and Dempsey (2014).

8. Calavita (2010).

9. Examples are Engel (1984), Sarat (1990), Ewick and Silbey (1998), and Gilliom (2001).

10. Examples are Bumiller (1992), McCann (1994), Morgan (1999), Engel and Munger (2003), and Marshall (2005).

11. Ewick and Silbey (1998).

12. Ibid., 45.

13. Examples are Ewick and Silbey (1998), Schneider (1986), and McCann (1994).

14. Schneider (1986).

15. Scheingold (2004).

16. Silbey (2005).

17. Ibid., 333.

18. Haltom and McCann (2004).

19. Gilliom (2001).

20. Ibid., p. 92.

21. Marshall (2005).

22. Ibid., 84.

23. Morgan (1999); Marshall and Barclay (2003); Albiston (2005, 2010).

24. Reese and Lindenberg (1998); Morgan (1999), Marshall (2005); Zippel (2004).

25. Munkres (2008); Seron, Pereira, and Kovath (2004); Hoffmann (2001).

26. Mason, Gouldon, and Wolfinger (2013).

27. Williams (2000, 2009).

28. Albiston (2010).

29. Ewick (2004, 85, emphasis mine).

30. Scheingold (2004, 14).

31. Haltom and McCann (2004).

32. Ibid., 21.

33. Ibid., 22.

34. Ibid.; Williams (2000).

35. Haltom and McCann (2004).

36. Ibid., 14.

37. Albiston (2010, 179).

38. Haltom and McCann (2004).

39. Examples are Olsen (1983), Pateman (1983), Elshtain (1981), Fineman and Mykitiuk (1994), Fineman (1995), Kessler (2001), Hochschild (2001, 2003), Williams (2000), and Williams and Cooper (2004)

40. Okin (1991, 124).

41. Doucet (2004, 2006).

42. Eisenstein (1988).

43. Williams (2000).

44. Smith (2003, 32).

45. Most notably, Mason, Wolfinger, and Goulden (2013).

46. For example, Ward and Wolf-Wendel (2012), and Evans and Grant (2008).

47. For example, Enloe (2014, 2015).

48. Marshall (2005); Albiston (2005, 2010); Reese and Lindenberg (2003); Zippel (2004), Munkres (2008); Seron, Pereira, and Kovath (2004); Hoffmann (2001).

49. Military ranks are often referenced by pay grade across the branches. An "E" designation indicates an enlisted rank, and an "O" designation indicates an officer rank. For a more comprehensive explanation of military ranks across service branches, see http://www.va.gov/vetsinworkplace/docs/em_rank.html.

50. Only one-third of the women in this study identified as being the primary breadwinner in her household. On a national level, by comparison, 40 percent of all households with children under age eighteen include mothers who

are the sole or primary breadwinner (Wang, Parker, and Taylor, 2013). However, the majority of women in my study (twenty-two of forty-eight) responded that they and their partner were "equal" breadwinners, which masks minor income differences that may bring my sample closer to the national average.

51. Schwartz-Shea and Yanow (2012).

Chapter 1

1. These case study chapters are by no means an exhaustive account of all of the data gathered in these interviews. Rather, they are an organized sampling of the most common and powerful themes as emphasized by the women themselves. Each of the themes raised here and in Chapter 2 is also, therefore, picked up and analyzed in more detail in the later chapters of this book.

2. The Pregnancy Discrimination Act of 1979 did, however, require than any workplace with a temporary disability program had to cover pregnancy in the same way it did other disabilities (Cantor et al. 2001)

3. Lenhoff and Bell (2013).

4. Haas (2004); Waldfogel (2001); Ray, Gornick, and Schmitt (2008).

5. 2011 Human Rights Watch.

6. Cantor et al. (2001).

7. Ibid.

8. Ray, Gornick, John Schmitt (2008).

9. Female service members are not covered under the FMLA. See Chapter 2 for a more complete discussion.

10. A stop-the-clock policy is one that is typically directed at faculty members who are on the tenure track. This policy would allow them to delay their tenure "clock." For example, if the faculty member has six years to prepare for tenure review, she or he could apply for an extension of this time line, typically for one year, when a major life event has occurred, such as the birth of a child.

11. Thornton (2005).

12. American Association of University Women (2004).

13. Hewlett (2002); Mason Wolfinger, and Goulden (2013); O'Brien Hallstein and O'Reilly (2012).

14. Townsend (2013); Mason et al. (2013).

15. Hewlett (2002).

16. Wolfinger et al. (2009).

17. O'Brien Hallstein and O'Reilly (2012).

18. Townsend (2013); Mason et al. (2013).

19. O'Brien Hallstein and O'Reilly (2012); Cooney and Uhlenberg (1989); Mason et al. (2006), and Wolfinger et al. 2009).

20. Wolfinger et al. (2009, 4).

21. *Mama, PhD* started out as a book of personal narratives edited by Elrina Evans and Caroline Grant, and later became a blog on the Inside Higher Ed website: http://www.insidehighered.com/blogs/mama-phd.

22. Ward and Wolf-Wendel (2012); Connelly and Ghodsee (2011); Mason et al. (2013).

23. Connelly and Ghodsee (2011).

24. COBRA is a federal provision allowing workers who lose their health benefits the right to continue those benefits for a short period of time. COBRA premiums are much higher than Paige's typical, university-subsidized premiums.

25. Kim (1999); Pleasance and Balmer (2012).

26. Hirsch and Lyons (2010); Albiston (2005, 2010); Payne-Pikus et al. (2010).

27. Albiston (2005, 27).

28. Payne-Pikus, Hagan, and Nelson (2010).

29. Examples are Engel (1984), Merry (1988), Sarat (1990), North (1990), Ewick and Silbey (1998), Engel and Munger (2003), and Albiston (2005, 2010).

30. Williams (2000, 2009).

31. Schrecker (2010).

32. This is consistent with other literature (e.g., Ward and Wold-Wendel 2012; Mason et al. 2013).

33. O'Brien Hallstein and O'Reilly (2012).

Chapter 2

1. For example, Miller and Williams (2001).

2. Francke (1997); Sadler (1997).

3. Women's Memorial Foundation (n.d.).

4. Weinstein and D'Amico (1999). Pfc. Jessica Lynch was revered as a "hero" in the U.S. media after becoming caught in a firefight while deployed in Iraq. Sustaining injuries and imprisonment, she was finally rescued and returned home a decorated veteran. Lynndie England was at the center of the Abu Ghraib prison scandal and photographed torturing Iraqi prisoners. Jennifer Lobasz (2008) has an excellent analysis of their media portrayal as gendered symbols in the media. Alexis Hutchinson was the single mother of a ten-month-old boy whose family care plan fell through, and she went AWOL as a result of not having anyone to care for him while her unit deployed to Iraq (Williams 2009). For a more detailed discussion of her treatment in the media as a gendered public identity, see Hampson (2011).

5. Major Mary Hegar, a helicopter pilot who was interviewed for local news station Freedom43TV in December 2012. http://freedom43tv.com/2012/12/05/military-women-suing-defense-department-for-ability-to-be-promoted/.

6. Lundquist (2008). Interestingly, her study shows that black men outstrip all other racial/ethnic and sex pairings in terms of their job satisfaction and that white women's satisfaction with their military jobs is the lowest of all groups.

7. Segal (1986).

8. Vinokur, Pierce, and Buck (1999).

9. Zellman et al. (2009).

10. Flake et al. (2009; Norris (2001).

11. Kelley et al. (2001).

12. Enloe (2007, 2014); Feinman (2000); Goldstein (2001); Higate (2003); Duncanson (2009); Taber (2011, 2013)

13. Taber (2013, 24).

14. Archer (2013).

15. Ibid.; Hampf (2004).

16. D'Amico (1998); Jeffreys (2007; Ensign (2004). It is worth noting that a recent spate of news stories regarding high-level cover-ups of sexual harassment in multiple military branches briefly brought this issue into the public spotlight in 2013 and again in 2014. Despite this, military leaders are still refusing to allow prosecutors, rather than military commanders, to investigate sexual assault in the military: attempts by some legislators to reform the military's sexual harassment procedures have failed in the Senate for two years in a row (McLaughlin 2013; Bassett 2014).

17. This began when women were first allowed to remain active duty once becoming pregnant, in the 1970s (Women's Memorial Foundation, n.d.). This leave was (and still officially is) known as "convalescent leave"—the length of which seems to have been initially at the discretion of commanding officers, but was for many years a set six weeks in all branches (with the exception of the Navy—see below), with the possibility of lengthening at the discretion of the chain of command. In early 2016, the Pentagon announced that all branches would now extend their maternity leave to twelve weeks for women and fourteen days of paid leave for fathers (Ferdinando 2016).

18. On July 2, 2015, the Navy announced that it was expanding paid maternity leave to eighteen weeks. The Pentagon's decision in early 2016 to grant women in all branches twelve weeks of paid leave superseded this policy, so that unless women in the Navy became pregnant within thirty days of the enactment of the latest policy, they are now subject to the twelve-week leave (Ferdinando 2016).

19. Hall and Spurlock (2013).

20. Roche-Paull (2013).

21. A system used by the military to determine what a service member should be expected to do mentally, physically, and medically for certain jobs and for their particular circumstances.

22. There are a few minor exceptions to this: some women were asked to report to sign paperwork after leaving the hospital but not specifically to work.

23. Merry (1990); McCann (1994).

24. Schneider (1986, 323).

25. Williams (1991).

26. Bumiller (1992); McCann (1994); Marshall (2005).

27. That was the case at the time of my interview with Zoe. It is worth noting, however, that the Air Force changed its policy in 2012 to extend this time period to twelve months postpartum for breast-feeding mothers. Until recently, the Army required postpartum mothers to be eligible to deploy as early as four months after giving birth. http://breastfeedingincombatboots. com/military-policies/.

28. Bumiller (1992); Morgan (1999); Quinn (2000); Marshall (2005).

29. Albiston (2005, 2010).)

30. Albiston (2005, 2010); Edelman, Erlanger, and Lande (1993); Edelman, Uggen, and Erlanger (1999); Yamada (2007); Skaggs (2008).

31. Powers (2011).

32 At the time I spoke with Chloe, the Army did not have a breast-feeding policy in its regulations (and was the only branch not to have one). However, the Army's "Guide to Female Soldier Readiness" did contain this "leader tip": "It is critical that leaders support their Soldiers. The ability to successfully continue breastfeeding after returning to work involves space, time, and support. Leaders need to provide female Soldiers with social and administrative support if the decision is made to continue breastfeeding after returning to work. Providing designated space in the workplace where mothers may express breast milk is important since many active duty mothers do not have private offices. If a designated room cannot be provided, the use of empty conference rooms or offices may suffice." In October 2015, the Army became the last branch of the U.S. military to implement formal guidelines for supporting nursing service members (Grinberg 2015).

Chapter 3

1. Marshall (2005); Albiston (2005, 2010); Hoffmann (2001).

2. Ewick and Silbey (1998); Sherwin (2000); Doyle (2003); Goodman (2006); Haltom and McCann (2004).

3. Sarat (1990); Gilliom (2001); Engel and Munger (2003).

4. Haltom and McCann (2004).

5. Heimer (1999); Quinn (2000).

6. Edelman et al. (1993); Marshall (2005).

7. Edelman and Suchman (1997).

8. Edelman (2004, 245).

9. Albiston (2005, 43).
10. Hirsch and Lyons (2010, 293).
11. Ewick and Silbey (1998, 220).
12. Sacks (1988).
13. Kellogg (2009).
14. Morgan (1999).
15. This is now twelve weeks for all branches. See notes 17 and 18 in Chapter 2.
16. AFIs are general types of formal regulations to which Air Force service members are subject.
17. Scheingold (2004).
18. Walsh (2010).
19. Harris-Lacewell (2006).

Chapter 4

1. For example, Levi (1997); Weingast (1995); Theriault (2006, 2008); Smith (2007).
2. Schmidt (2011); Scott (1995); Powell and DiMaggio (1991); March and Olsen (1989).
3. Marshall (2005); Gilliom (2001); Morgan (1999); McCann (1994); Albiston (2005, 2010).
4. Schmidt (2011, 48).
5. Kulawik (2009).
6. Schmidt (2008, 2011).
7. Schmidt (2011, 61).
8. Lawrence, Suddaby, and Leca (2009).
9. See also Wetherell, Taylor, and Yates (2001); Powell and Dimaggio (1991); Phillips, Lawrence, and Hardy (2004); Kulawik (2009).
10. Carmichael (1988).
11. Béland (2009); Blyth (2002); Schmidt (2002); Cox (2001).

Chapter 5

1. Albiston (2010); Quinn (2000); Scheingold (2004]); McCann (1994); Bumiller (1992); Ewick (2004); Ewick and Silbey (1998); Marshall (2005); Gruber (1998); Williams and Cooper (2004).
2. Minow (1999); Gustafson (2011); Gilliom (200); Nussbaum (2004); Bumiller (2008); Sigal and Jacobsen (1999); Hancock (2004); Jordan-Zachery (2008); Gilens (2000).
3. Hancock (2004).
4. Roberts (1997); Jordan-Zachery (2008).

5. de Silva de Alwis (2011); Williams (2000); Tinkler (2012).

6. Berns (2002); Williams (2000, 2009); Williams and Cooper (2004); Fuegen et al. (2004); Kessler-Harris (2001); Kelly et al. (2010).

7. Williams (2000).

8. For instance, Williams (2000) cites a *Washington Post* poll from 1998 indicating that two-thirds of Americans believe it would be better for women to stay home and care for family and children. Yet this ideology is not time-bound. In a Pew Center study twelve years later, 37 percent of respondents said that "mothers of young children working outside the home" is a "bad thing for society" while only 27 percent of respondents said it is a "good thing for society" (Taylor et al. 2010).

9. Okin (1991)

10. Fineman (1995).

11. Kessler (2001).

12. Brandth and Kvande (1998); Doucet (2004, 2006); Wall and Arnold (2007).

13. Doucet (2004, 2006); Featherstone (2003).

14. Hobson (2002); Jesmin and Seward (2011); Haas and O'Brien (2010); McKay and Doucet (2010).

15. U.S. Bureau of Labor and Statistics (2011). It is worth noting, however, that men were 1.4 times more likely than women (2.6 percent of those taking leave, compared to 1.9 percent of women taking leave) to cite child or elder care (other than for illness) as their reason for taking leave.

16. Townsend (2013); Krapf et al. (2014).

17. Hochschild (2003); Mason, Wolfinger, and Goulden (2013); Townsend 2013); Krapf et al. (2014).

18. Enloe (2000)

19. Ibid., 37.

20. The length of time depends on the service branch and whether the mother is breast-feeding. The Air Force recently expanded this time to twelve months for breast-feeding mothers, but at the time the interviews were conducted, the women in this study were eligible for four to six months of postpartum deferral. See notes 17 and 18 in Chapter 2 for further details.

21. A profile is a system used by the military to determine what a service member should be expected to do mentally, physically and medically for certain jobs and for their particular circumstances. A pregnancy changes an individual's profile temporarily. See Chapter 2 for more discussion of profiles.

22. "Punch out" is slang for ejecting from a military aircraft.

23. Mason et al. (2013); Wolfinger Mason, and Goulden (2009); Krapf, Ursprung, and Zimmermann (2014).

24. Declercq et al. (2013).

25. Both the use of contraception and abortion are forbidden under the teachings of the Catholic Church. Marie chose to use contraception because she felt that if she were to become pregnant, she would have to give up her career because the constraints of being a mother in academia would be too great. Additionally, because of her religion, abortion is an unthinkable option for Marie.

26. "Packet" refers to the packet of materials a tenure-track professor is required to put together in order to support a case for tenure. These materials include published materials, teaching evaluations, and other evidence of meeting the tenure criteria specified by the tenure-granting institution.

27. Albiston (2005, 17). See also Albiston (2010).

28. Tushnet (1984, 1380).

Chapter 6

1. Fineman (1995).

2. Littleton ([1987] 1991).

3. Kay (2002, 328).

4. Examples are Elshtain (1993), Okin (1991), and Kessler (2001).

5. Hochschild (2001, 2003).

6. Curtis (2011).

7. Mason et al. (2013, 84).

8. CNN (2013).

9. Mason et al. (2013); Townsend (2013); O'Brien Hallstein and O'Reilly (2012); Thornton (2005); Haas (2004); Hewlett (2002); Vinokur, Pierce, and Buck (1999); Waldfogel (1998, 2001); Cooney and Uhlenberg (1989).

10. Notable exceptions include Williams (2009) and Kelly et al. (2010).

11. Pheterson's (1986) article offers an excellent discussion of the concepts of "internalized oppression" and "internalized domination" in the contexts of race, gender, ethnicity, and class: "Internalized domination perpetuates oppression of others and alienation from oneself by either denying or degrading all but a narrow range of human possibilities" (148).

12. Sandberg (2013, 26)

13. Leanse (2014).

14. As of January 2016, the Pentagon extended paternity leave for all branches of service to fourteen days (Ryan 2016).

15. Klerman, Daley, and Pozniak (2012).

16. Mandy was not targeted by the recruitment techniques in this study, since she is not a member of the faculty at Elm. She is therefore also not included in the official statistics on the women faculty participants listed in other parts of this book, including Chapter 1. However, when she saw my recruitment e-mail, Mandy contacted me and requested to participate anyway. I include

her comments here, since she was one of the few participants who raised the possibility of mandatory leave, and she did so quite eloquently.

17. Sweden recently extended this policy, requiring that in 2016, the period of paid leave for men be extended to three months (as reported by the *Guardian*, May 28, 2015).

18. Bennhold (2010); Hansegard (2012); Theodossiou (2012).

19. Martinez (2015).

20. World Bank (2015).

21. Williams (1987, 431)

22. Though I would be remiss if I did not recognize that the United States is notoriously ungenerous in its work/life balance laws and policies. Undoubtedly, were the country to implement policies such as those in Sweden, or indeed even paid family leave, then many women would report experiencing greater success at achieving work/life balance. Doubtless, too, we would see an improvement in women's participation and retention in the workplace, such as other countries, with more generous leave policies, experience.

23. Epp (2009).

24. For an in-depth critique of *Lean In,* see bell hooks's article, "Dig Deep: Beyond Lean In" (2013). To her credit, in a long post on Facebook, Sheryl Sandberg recently acknowledged that "leaning in" is harder for some than for others: "Before, I did not quite get it. I did not realize how hard it is to succeed at work when you are overwhelmed at home." She went on to call for better laws and policies aimed at supporting working mothers and to recognize that single mothers in particular need "more supportive communities" (Sandberg 2016).

Works Cited

Albiston, Catherine R. 2005. "Bargaining in the Shadow of Social Institutions: Competing Discourses and Social Change in Workplace Mobilization of Civil Rights." *Law and Society Review* 39(1): 11–50.

———. 2010. *Institutional Inequality and the Mobilization of the Family and Medical Leave Act: Rights on Leave.* Cambridge: Cambridge University Press.

American Association of University Women. 2004. *Tenure Denied: Cases of Sex Discrimination in Academia.* Washington, DC: AAUW Educational Foundation and AAUW Legal Advocacy Fund

Archer, Emerald M. 2013. "The Power of Gendered Stereotypes in the US Marine Corps." *Armed Forces and Society* 39(2): 359–91.

Bassett, Laura. 2014. "Gillibrand's Military Sexual Assault Reform Fails Senate." *Huffington Post.* http://www.huffingtonpost.com/2014/03/06/ gillibrands-military-sexual-assault_n_4913108.html (accessed October 7, 2016).

Béland, Daniel. 2009. "Ideas, Institutions, and Policy Change." *Journal of European Public Policy* 16(5): 701–18.

Bennhold, Katrin. 2010. "In Sweden, Men Can Have It All." *New York Times,* June 9. http://www.nytimes.com/2010/06/10/world/europe/10iht-sweden. htmlaccessed February 15, 2013).

Berns, Sandra. 2002. *Women Going Backwards: Law and Change in a Family Unfriendly Society.* Aldershot: Ashgate.

Blyth, Mark. 2002. *Great Transformations: Economic Ideas and Institutional Change in the Twentieth Century.* New York: Cambridge University Press.

Brandth, Berit, and Elin Kvande. 1998. "Masculinity and Child Care: The Reconstruction of Fathering." *Sociological Review* 46(2): 293–313.

Bumiller, Kristin. 1992. *The Civil Rights Society: The Social Construction of Victims.* Baltimore: Johns Hopkins University Press.

———. 2008. *In an Abusive State: How Neoliberalism Appropriated the Feminist Movement against Sexual Violence.* Durham: Duke University Press.

Calavita, Kitty. 2010. *Invitation to Law and Society: An Introduction to the Study of Real Law.* Chicago: University of Chicago Press.

Cantor, David, Jane Waldfogel, Jeffrey Kerwin, Mareena McKinley Wright, Kerry Levin, John Rauch, Tracey Hagerty, and Martha Stapleton Kudela. 2001. *Balancing the Needs of Families and Employers: Family and Medical Leave Surveys.* Rockville, MD: Westat.

Carmichael, H. Lorne. 1988. "Incentives in Academics: Why Is There Tenure?" *Journal of Political Economy* 96(3): 453–72.

CNN Staff. 2013. "By the Numbers: Women in the U.S. Military." *CNN U.S.*, January 24. http://www.cnn.com/2013/01/24/us/military-women-glance/ (accessed February 20, 2014).

Cohn, D'Vera, Gretchen Livingston and Wendy Wang, 2014, "After Decades of Decline, a Rise in Stay-at-Home Mothers." Washington, DC: Pew Research Center's Social and Demographic Trends project, April.

Connelly, Rachel, and Kristen Rogheh Ghodsee. 2011. *Professor Mommy: Finding Work-Family Balance in Academia.* Lanham, MD: Rowman & Littlefield.

Cooney, Teresa M., and Peter Uhlenberg. 1989. "Family-Building Patterns of Professional Women: A Comparison of Lawyers, Physicians, and Postsecondary Teachers." *Journal of Marriage and Family* 51(3): 749–58.

Cox, Robert Henry. 2001. "The Social Construction of an Imperative: Why Welfare Reform Happened in Denmark and the Netherlands But Not in Germany." *World Politics* 53(3): 463–98.

Curtis, John W. 2011. *Persistent Inequity: Gender and Academic Employment.* Washington DC: AAUP.

D'Amico, Francine. 1998. "Feminist Perspectives on Women Warriors." In *The Women and War Reader*, ed. Lois Ann Lorentzen, and Jennifer Turpin, 119–25. New York: New York University Press.

Declercq, Eugene R., Carol Sakala, Maureen P. Corry, Sandra Applebaum, and Ariel Herrlich. 2013. *Listening to Mothers III: New Mothers Speak Out: Major Survey Findings.* New York: Childbirth Connection.

De Silva de Alwis, Rangita. 2010. "Examining Gender Stereotypes in New Work/Family Reconciliation Policies: The Creation of a New Paradigm for Egalitarian Legislation." *Duke Journal of Gender Law and Policy* 18:305.

Doucet, Andrea. 2004. "Fathers and the Responsibility for Children: A Puzzle and a Tension." *Atlantis: Critical Studies in Gender, Culture and Social Justice* 28(2): 103–14.

———. 2006. *Do Men Mother? Fathering, Care, and Domestic Responsibility.* Toronto: University of Toronto Press.

Doyle, Aaron. 2003. *Arresting Images: Crime and Policing in Front of the Television Camera.* Toronto: University of Toronto Press.

Duncanson, Claire. 2009. "Forces for Good? Narratives of Military Masculinity in Peacekeeping Operations." *International Feminist Journal of Politics* 11(1): 63–80.

Edelman, Lauren B. 2004. "The Legal Lives of Private Organizations." In *The Blackwell Companion to Law and Society*, ed. Austin Sarat, 231–52. Malden, MA: Blackwell.

Edelman, Lauren B., Howard S. Erlanger, and John Lande. 1993. "Internal Dispute Resolution: The Transformation of Civil Rights in the Workplace." *Law and Society Review* 27(3): 497–534.

Edelman, Lauren B., and Mark C. Suchman. 1997. "The Legal Environments of Organizations." *Annual Review of Sociology* 23:479–515.

Edelman, Lauren B., Christopher Uggen, and Howard S. Erlanger. 1999. "The Endogeneity of Legal Regulation: Grievance Procedures as Rational Myth." *American Journal of Sociology* 105(2): 406–54.

Eisenstein, Zillah R. 1990. *The Female Body and the Law*. Berkeley: University of California Press.

Elshtain, Jean Bethke. 1981. *Public Man, Private Woman: Women in Social and Political Thought*. Princeton: Princeton University Press.

Engel, David M. 1984. "The Oven Bird's Song: Insiders, Outsiders, and Personal Injuries in an American Community." *Law and Society Review* 18(4): 551–82.

Engel, David M., and Frank W. Munger. 2003. *Rights of Inclusion: Law and Identity in the Life Stories of Americans with Disabilities*. Chicago: University of Chicago Press.

Enloe, Cynthia H. 2007. *Globalization and Militarization: Feminists Make the Link*. Lanham, MD: Rowman & Littlefield.

———. 2014. *Bananas, Beaches and Bases: Making Feminist Sense of International Politics*. 2nd ed. Berkeley: University of California Press.

———. 2015. "The Recruiter and the Sceptic: A Critical Feminist Approach to Military Studies." *Critical Military Studies* 1(1): 3–10.

Ensign, Tod. 2006. *America's Military Today: The Challenge of Militarism*. New York: New Press.

Epp, Charles R. 2010. *Making Rights Real: Activists, Bureaucrats, and the Creation of the Legalistic State*. Chicago: University of Chicago Press.

Evans, Elrena, and Caroline Grant. 2008. *Mama: PhD Women Write about Motherhood and Academic Life*. New Brunswick, NJ: Rutgers University Press.

Ewick, Patricia. 2004. "Consciousness and Ideology." In *The Blackwell Companion to Law and Society*, ed. Austin Sarat. Malden, MA: Blackwell.

Ewick, Patricia, and Susan S. Silbey. 1998. *The Common Place of Law: Stories from Everyday Life*. Chicago: University of Chicago Press. Featherstone,

Brid. 2003. "Taking Fathers Seriously." *British Journal of Social Work* 33(2):
239–54.

Feinman, Ilene Rose. 2000. *Citizenship Rites: Feminist Soldiers and Feminist
Antimilitarists*. New York: New York University Press.

Ferdinando, Lisa. 2016. "Carter Announces Twelve Weeks Paid Military
Maternity Leave, Other Benefits." *DOD News*. http://www.defense.gov/
News/Article/Article/645958/carter-announces-12-weeks-paid-military-
maternity-leave-other-benefits (accessed October 7, 2016).

Fineman, Martha Albertson. 1995. *The Neutered Mother, the Sexual Family
and Other Twentieth Century Tragedies*. New York: Routledge.

Fineman, Martha A., and Roxanne Mykitiuk. 1994. *The Public Nature of Private Violence: The Discovery of the Domestic Abuse*. New York: Routledge.

Flake, Eric M., Beth Ellen Davis, Patti L. Johnson, and Laura S. Middleton.
2009. "The Psychosocial Effects of Deployment on Military Children."
Journal of Developmental and Behavioral Pediatrics 30(4): 271–78.

Francke, Linda Bird. 1997. *Ground Zero: The Gender Wars in the Military*.
New York: Simon & Schuster.

Fuegen, Kathleen, Monica Biernat, Elizabeth Haines, and Kay Deaux. 2004.
"Mothers and Fathers in the Workplace: How Gender and Parental Status
Influence Judgments of Job-Related Competence." *Journal of Social Issues*
60(4): 737–54.

Gilens, Martin. 2000. *Why Americans Hate Welfare: Race, Media, and the
Politics of Antipoverty Policy*. Chicago: University of Chicago Press.

Gilliom, John. 2001. *Overseers of the Poor: Surveillance, Resistance, and the
Limits of Privacy*. Chicago: University of Chicago Press.

Goldstein, Joshua S. 2001. *War and Gender: How Gender Shapes the War
System and Vice Versa*. Cambridge: Cambridge University Press.

Goodman, Douglas J. 2006. "Approaches to Law and Popular Culture." *Law
and Social Inquiry* 31:757–84.

Grinberg, Emanuella. 2015. "Army Issues New Breastfeeding Policy." *CNN.
com* http://www.cnn.com/2015/10/02/living/army-breastfeeding-policy-
feat/ (accessed October 7, 2016).

Gruber, James E. 1998. "The Impact of Male Work Environments and
Organizational Policies on Women's Experiences of Sexual Harassment."
Gender and Society 12(3): 301–20.

Gustafson, Kaaryn S. 2011. *Cheating Welfare: Public Assistance and the Crimi-
nalization of Poverty*. New York: New York University Press.

Haas, Linda. 2004. "Parental Leave and Gender Equality: What Can the
United States Learn from the European Union?" In *Equality in the Work-
place: Gendering Workplace Policy Analysis*, ed. Heidi Gottfried, and Laura
Reese,183–214. Lanham, MD: Lexington Books.

Haas, Linda, and Margaret O'Brien. 2010. "New Observations on How Fathers Work and Care: Introduction to the Special Issue-Men, Work and Parenting-Part I." *Fathering* 8(3): 271.

Hall, Katy, and Chris Spurlock. 2013. "Paid Parental Leave: U.S. vs. the World." *Huffington Post*, February 4. http://www.huffingtonpost. com/2013/02/04/maternity-leave-paid-parental-leave-_n_2617284.html (accessed July 22, 2013).

Haltom, William, and Michael McCann. 2004. *Distorting the Law: Politics, Media, and the Litigation Crisis*. Chicago: University of Chicago Press.

Hampf, M. Michaela. 2004. "'Dykes' or 'Whores': Sexuality and the Women's Army Corps in the United States during World War II." *Women's Studies International Forum* 27(1): 13–30.

Hampson, Sarah Cote. 2011. "Framing Mothers in Uniform: Public Discourse and Policy in the Case of Army Specialist Alexis Hutchinson." Paper presented at the Law and Society Annual Meeting, San Francisco, June.

Hancock, Ange-Marie. 2004. *The Politics of Disgust: The Public Identity of the Welfare Queen*. New York: New York University Press.

Hansegard, Jens. 2012. "For Paternity Leave, Sweden Asks If Two Months Is Enough." *Wall Street Journal*, July 31. online.wsj.com/article/SB100008723 9639044422690457756110002033684.html (accessed February 15, 2013).

Harris-Lacewell, Melissa Victoria. 2006. *Barbershops, Bibles, and BET: Everyday Talk and Black Political Thought*. Princeton: Princeton University Press.

Heilman, Madeline E., and Julie J. Chen. 2005. "Same Behavior, Different Consequences: Reactions to Men's and Women's Altruistic Citizenship Behavior." *Journal of Applied Psychology* 90(3): 431–41.

Heimer, Carol A. 1999. "Competing Institutions: Law, Medicine, and Family in Neonatal Intensive Care." *Law and Society Review* 33(1): 17–66.

Hewlett, Sylvia Ann. 2002. *Creating a Life: Professional Women and the Quest for Children*. New York: Talk Miramax Books.

Higate, Paul. 2003. *Military Masculinities: Identity and the State*. Westport, CT: Praeger.

Hirsch, Elizabeth, and Christopher J. Lyons. 2010. "Perceiving Discrimination on the Job: Legal Consciousness, Workplace Context, and the Construction of Race Discrimination." *Law and Society Review* 44(2): 269–98.

Hobson, Barbara Meil. 2002. *Making Men into Fathers: Men, Masculinities, and the Social Politics of Fatherhood*. Cambridge: Cambridge University Press.

Hochschild, Arlie Russell. 2001. *The Time Bind*. New York: Owl book.

Hochschild, Arlie Russell, with Anne Machung. 2003. *The Second Shift*, 2nd ed. New York: Penguin Books.

Hoffman, Elizabeth A. 2001. "Confrontation and Compromise: Dispute Resolution at a Worker Cooperative Coal Mine." *Law and Social Inquiry* 26:150–70.

hooks, bell. 2013. "Dig Deep: Beyond Lean In." *Feminist Wire*, October 28. http://www.thefeministwire.com/2013/10/17973/ (accessed October 7, 2016).

Human Rights Watch. 2011. *Failing Its Families: Lack of Paid Leave and Work-Family Supports in the U.S.* New York: Human Rights Watch.

Jeffreys, Sheila. 2007. "Double Jeopardy: Women, the US Military and the War in Iraq." *Women's Studies International Forum* 30(1): 16–25.

Jesmin, Syeda S., and Rudy Ray Seward. 2011. "Parental Leave and Fathers' Involvement with Children in Bangladesh: A Comparison with United States." *Journal of Comparative Family Studies* 42(1): 95–112.

Jordan-Zachery, Julia S. 2008. *Black Women, Cultural Images and Social Policy.* New York: Routledge.

Kay, Herma Hill. 2002. "Equality and Difference: The Case of Pregnancy." In *Gender and Law: Theory, Doctrine and Commentary*, ed. Katherine T. Bartlett, Angela P. Harris, and Deborah L. Rhode. New York: Aspen.

Kelley, Michelle L., Ellen Hock, Jennifer F. Bonney, and Monica A. Gaffney. 2001. "Navy Mothers Experiencing and Not Experiencing Deployment: Reasons for Staying In or Leaving the Military." *Military Psychology* 13(1): 55–71.

Kellogg, Katherine C. 2009. "Operating Room: Relational Spaces and Micro-institutional Change in Surgery." *American Journal of Sociology* 115(3): 657–711.

Kelly, Erin L., Samantha K. Ammons, Kelly Chermack, and Phyllis Moen. 2010. "Gendered Challenge, Gendered Response Confronting the Ideal Worker Norm in a White-Collar Organization." *Gender and Society* 24(3): 281–303.

Kessler, Laura T. 2001. "The Attachment Gap: Employment Discrimination Law, Women's Cultural Caregiving, and the Limits of Economic and Liberal Legal Theory." *University of Michigan Journal of Law Reform* 34:371–468.

Kessler-Harris, Alice. 2001. *In Pursuit of Equity: Women, Men, and the Quest for Economic Citizenship in 20th-Century America.* New York: Oxford University Press.

Kim, Pauline T. 1999. "Norms, Learning, and Law: Exploring the Influences on Workers." *University of Illinois Law Review* 2:447–516.

Klerman, Jacob Alex, Kelly Daley, and Alyssa Pozniak. 2012. "Family and Medical Leave in 2012: Technical Report." Cambridge, MA: Abt

Associates. https://www.dol.gov/asp/evaluation/fmla/fmla-2012-technical-report.pdf.

Krapf, Matthias, Heinrich Ursprung, and Christian Zimmermann. 2014. *Parenthood and Productivity of Highly Skilled Labor: Evidence from the Groves of Academe.* St. Louis: Federal Reserve Bank of St. Louis.

Kulawik, Teresa. 2009. "Staking the Frame of a Feminist Discursive Institutionalism." *Politics and Gender* 5(2): 262–71.

Lawrence, Thomas B., Roy Suddaby, and Bernard Leca. 2009. *Institutional Work : Actors and Agency in Institutional Studies of Organizations.* Cambridge: Cambridge University Press.

Leanse, Ellen Petry. 2014. "'Just' Say No Women 2.0." Women 2.0, February 17, 2014. http://women2.com/2014/02/17/just-say/ (accessed June 11, 2016).

Lenhoff, Donna R., and Lissa Bell. 2013. *Government Support for Working Families and for Communities: Family and Medical Leave as a Case Study.* Washington, DC: National Partnership for Women and Families. http://www.nationalpartnership.org/research-library/work-family/fmla/fmla-case-study-lenhoff-bell.pdf.

Levi, Margaret. 1997. "A Model, a Method, and a Map: Rational Choice in Comparative and Historical Analysis." In *Comparative Politics: Rationality, Culture, and Structure,* ed. Mark Irving Lichbach and Alan S. Zuckerman. New York: Cambridge University Press.

Lobasz, Jennifer K. 2008. "The Woman in Peril and the Ruined Woman: Representations of Female Soldiers in the Iraq War." *Journal of Women, Politics and Policy* 29(3): 305–34.

Lundquist, Jennifer Hickes. 2008. "Ethnic and Gender Satisfaction in the Military: The Effect of a Meritocratic Institution." *American Sociological Review* 73(3): 477–96.

March, James G., and Johan P. Olsen. 1989. *Rediscovering Institutions: The Organizational Basis of Politics.* New York: Free Press.

Marshall, Anna-Maria. 2005. "Idle Rights: Employees' Rights Consciousness and the Construction of Sexual Harassment Policies." *Law and Society Review* 39:83–124.

Marshall, Anna-Maria, and Scott Barclay. 2003. "In Their Own Words: How Ordinary People Construct the Legal World." *Law and Social Inquiry* 28(3): 617–28.

Martinez, Michael. 2015. "Dads Cherish Swedish Parental Leave." *CNN.com,* April 5. http://www.cnn.com/2015/04/05/living/cnnphotos-swedish-dads-parental-leave/ (accessed July 8, 2015).

Mason, Mary Ann, Mark Gouldon, and N. H. Wolfinger. 2006. "Babies Matter: Pushing the Gender Equity Revolution Forward." In *The*

Balancing Act: Gendered Perspectives in Faculty Roles and Work Lives, ed. S. J. Bracken, J. K. Allen, and D. R. Dean. Sterling, VA: Stylus.

Mason, Mary Ann, Nicholas H Wolfinger, and Marc Goulden. 2013. *Do Babies Matter? Gender and Family in the Ivory Tower*. New Brunswick, NJ: Rutgers University Press

McCann, Michael W. 1994. *Rights at Work: Pay Equity Reform and the Politics of Legal Mobilization*. Chicago: University of Chicago Press.

McKay, Lindsey, and Andrea Doucet. 2010. "'Without Taking Away Her Leave': A Canadian Case Study of Couples' Decisions on Fathers' Use of Paid Parental Leave." *Fathering: A Journal of Theory, Research, and Practice about Men as Fathers* 8(3): 300–20.

McLaughlin, Elliot C. 2013. "Military Chiefs Oppose Removing Commanders from Sexual Assault Probes." *CNN*. June 4. http://www.cnn.com/2013/06/04/politics/senate-hearing-military-sexual-assault/index.html.

Merry, Sally Engle. 1988. "Legal Pluralism." *Law and Society Review* 22(5): 869–96.

——— 1990. *Getting Justice and Getting Even : Legal Consciousness among Working-Class Americans*. Chicago: University of Chicago Press.

Miller, Laura J., and John Allen Williams. 2001. "Do Military Policies on Gender and Sexuality Undermine Combat Effectiveness?" In *Soldiers and Civilians: The Civil-Military Gap and Americans National Security*, ed. Peter D. Feaver, and Richard H. Kohn, 361–402. Cambridge, MA: MIT Press.

Minow, Martha. 1999. *Not Only for Myself: Identity, Politics, and the Law*. New York: New Press.

Morgan, Phoebe A. 1999. "Risking Relationships: Understanding the Litigation Choices of Sexually Harassed Women." *Law and Society Review* 33(1): 67–92.

Munkres, Susan A. 2008. "Claiming 'Victim' to Harassment Law: Legal Consciousness of the Privileged." *Law and Social Inquiry* 33(2): 447–72.

Norris, Deborah. 2001. "Working Them Out . . . Working Them In: Ideology and the Everyday Lives of Female Military Partners Experiencing the Cycle of Deployment." *Atlantis: Critical Studies in Gender, Culture and Social Justice* 26(1): 55–64.

North, Douglass C. 1990. *Institutions, Institutional Change, and Economic Performance*. Cambridge: Cambridge University Press.

Nussbaum, Martha Craven. 2004. *Hiding from Humanity: Disgust, Shame, and the Law*. Princeton: Princeton University Press.

O'Brien Hallstein, Lynn, and Andrea O'Reilly. 2012. "Academic Motherhood in a Post–Second Wave Context: Framing the Conversation." In *Academic*

Motherhood in a Post–Second Wave Context: Challenges, Strategies, and Possibilities, ed. Lynn O'Brien Hallstein and Andrea O'Reilly. Bradford, ON: Demeter Press.

Okin, Susan Moller. 1991. *Justice, Gender, and the Family*. New York: Basic Books.

Olsen, Frances E. 1983. "The Family and the Market: A Study of Ideology and Legal Reform." *Harvard Law Review* 96(7): 1497–1578.

Pateman, Carol. 1983. "Feminist Critiques of the Public/Private Dichotomy." In *Private and Public in Social Life*, ed. Stanley Benn and Gerald Gaus, 281–300. London: Croom Helm.

Payne-Pikus, Monique R., John Hagan, and Robert L. Nelson. 2010. "Experiencing Discrimination: Race and Retention in America's Largest Law Firms." *Law and Society Review* 44(3–4): 553–84.

Pew Research Center. 2015. *Raising Kids and Running a Household: How Working Parents Share the Load*. November. http://www.pewsocialtrends. org/2015/11/04/raising-kids-and-running-a-household-how-working-parents-share-the-load/

Pheterson, Gail. 1986. "Alliances between Women: Overcoming Internalized Oppression and Internalized Domination." *Signs* 12(1): 146–60.

Phillips, Nelson, Thomas B. Lawrence, and Cynthia Hardy. 2004. "Discourse and Institutions." *Academy of Management Review* 29(4): 635–52.

Pleasence, Pascoe, and Nigel J. Balmer. 2012. "Ignorance in Bliss: Modeling Knowledge of Rights in Marriage and Cohabitation." *Law and Society Review* 46(2): 297–333.

Powell, Walter W., and Paul DiMaggio. 1991. *The New Institutionalism in Organizational Analysis*. Chicago: University of Chicago Press.

Powers, Rod. 2011. *Basic Training for Dummies*. Hoboken, NJ: Wiley.

Quinn, Beth A. 2000. "The Paradox of Complaining: Law, Humor, and Harassment in the Everyday Work World." *Law and Social Inquiry* 25(4): 1151–85.

Ray, Rebecca, Janet C. Gornick, and John Schmitt. 2008. *Parental Leave Policies in 21 Countries—Assessing Generosity and Gender Equality*. Washington, DC: Center for Economic and Policy Research.

Reese, Laura A., and Karen E. Lindenberg. 2003. "The Importance of Training on Sexual Harassment Policy Outcomes." *Review of Public Personnel Administration* 23(3): 175–91.

Roberts, Dorothy E. 1997. *Killing the Black Body: Race, Reproduction, and the Meaning of Liberty*. New York: Vintage books.

Roche-Paull, Robyn. 2013. "Military Breastfeeding Policies." http://breast-feedingincombatboots.com/military-policies/.

Ryan, Missy. 2016. "Pentagon Extends Maternity and Paternity Leave for Military Families." *Washington Post*, January 28. https://www.washingtonpost.com/news/checkpoint/wp/2016/01/28/pentagon-extends-maternity-and-paternity-leave-for-military-families/.

Sacks, Karen. 1988. *Caring by the Hour: Women, Work, and Organizing at Duke Medical Center*. Champaign: University of Illinois Press.

Sadler, Georgia Clark. 1997. "Women in Combat: The U.S. Military and the Impact of the Persian Gulf War." In *Wives and Warriors: Women and the Military in the United States and Canada*, ed. Laurie Weinstein and Christie C. White, 79–99. Westport, CT: Bergin and Garvey.

Sandberg, Sheryl. 2013. *Lean in: Women, Work, and the Will to Lead*. New York: Knopf.

———. 2016. Facebook post. May 6. https://www.facebook.com/sheryl/posts/10156819553860177.

Sarat, Austin. 1990. "Law Is All Over: The Power, Resistance and the Legal Consciousness of the Welfare Poor." *Yale Journal of Law and the Humanities* 2:343–79.

Scheingold, Stuart A. 2004. *The Politics of Rights: Lawyers, Public Policy, and Political Change*, 2nd ed. Ann Arbor: University of Michigan Press.

Schmidt, Vivien A. 2002. "Does Discourse Matter in the Politics of Welfare State Adjustment?" *Comparative Political Studies* 35(2): 168–93.

———. 2008. "Discursive Institutionalism: The Explanatory Power of Ideas and Discourse." *Annual Review of Political Science* 11(1): 303–26.

———. 2011. "Reconciling Ideas and Institutions through Discursive Institutionalism." In *Ideas and Politics in Social Science Research*, ed. Daniel Beland and Robert Henry Cox, 47–64. New York: Oxford University Press.

Schneider, Elizabeth M. 1986. "The Dialectic of Rights and Politics: Perspectives from the Women's Movement." *New York University Law Review* 61:589–652.

Schrecker, Ellen. 2010. *The Lost Soul of Higher Education: Corporatization, the Assault on Academic Freedom, and the End of the American University*. New York: New Press.

Schwartz-Shea, Peregrine, and Dvora Yanow. 2012. *Interpretive Research Design: Concepts and Processes*. New York: Routledge.

Scott, W. Richard. 1995. *Institutions and Organizations: Ideas, Interests and Identities*. Los Angeles: Sage.

Segal, Mady Wechsler. 1986. "The Military and the Family as Greedy Institutions." *Armed Forces and Society* 13(1): 9–38.

Seron, Carroll, Joseph Pereira, and Jean Kovath. 2004. "Judging Police Misconduct: 'Street-Level' versus Professional Policing." *Law and Society Review* 38(4): 665–710.

Sherwin, Richard K. 2000. *When Law Goes Pop: The Vanishing Line between Law and Popular Culture.* Chicago: University of Chicago Press.

Sigal, Janet, and Heidi Jacobsen. 1999. "A Cross-Cultural Exploration of Factors Affecting Reactions to Sexual Harassment: Attitudes and Policies." *Psychology, Public Policy, and Law* 5(3): 760–85.

Silbey, Susan S. 2005. "After Legal Consciousness." *Annual Review of Law and Social Science* 1(1): 323–68.

Skaggs, Sheryl. 2008. "Producing Change or Bagging Opportunity? The Effects of Discrimination Litigation on Women in Supermarket Management." *American Journal of Sociology* 113(4): 1148–82.

Smith, Patricia. 2003. "Autonomy, Aspiration, and Accomplishment: Some Steps and Barriers to Equality for Women." In *Feminist Legal Theory: An Anti-Essentialist Reader,* ed. Nancy E. Dowd and Michelle S. Jacobs, 26–33. New York: New York University Press.

Smith, Steven S. 2007. *Party Influence in Congress.* Cambridge: Cambridge University Press.

Taber, Nancy. 2011. "'You Better Not Get Pregnant While You're Here': Tensions between Masculinities and Femininities in Military Communities of Practice." *International Journal of Lifelong Education* 30(3): 331–48.

———. 2013. "A Composite Life History of a Mother in the Military: Storying Gendered Experiences." *Women's Studies International Forum* 37:16–25.

Taylor, Paul, Kim Parker, Wendy Wang, Richard Morin, Juliana Menasce Horowitz, D'Vera Cohn, and Gretchen Livingston. 2010. *The Decline of Marriage and Rise of New Families.* Washington, DC: Pew Research Center. http://www.pewsocialtrends.org/files/2010/11/pew-social-trends-2010-families.pdf.

Theodossiou, Eleni. 2012. *U.S. Labor Market Shows Gradual Improvement in 2011.* Washington, DC: US Department of Labor.

Theriault, Sean M. 2006. "Party Polarization in the US Congress: Member Replacement and Member Adaptation." *Party Politics* 12(4): 483–503.

———. 2008. *Party Polarization in Congress.* Cambridge: Cambridge University Press.

Thornton, Saranna. 2005. "The Challenge of Balancing Careers and Family Work." *New Directions for Higher Education* 130 (Summer): 81–90.

Tinkler, Justine E. 2012. "Resisting the Enforcement of Sexual Harassment Law." *Law and Social Inquiry* 37(1): 1–24.

Townsend, Robert B. 2013. "Gender and Success in Academia: More from the Historians' Career Paths Survey." *Perspectives on History* 51(1). https://www.historians.org/publications-and-directories/perspectives-on-history/january-2013/gender-and-success-in-academia# (accessed October 7, 2016).

Tushnet, Mark. 1984. "A Critique of Rights: An Essay on Rights." *Texas Law Review* 62(8): 1363–1404.

U.S. Bureau of Labor and Statistics. 2011. *Economic News Release*, October 17. http://www.bls.gov/news.release/famee.to6.htm.

Vinokur, Amiram D., Penny F. Pierce, and Catherine L. Buck. 1999. "Work-Family Conflicts of Women in the Air Force: Their Influence on Mental Health and Functioning." *Journal of Organizational Behavior* 20(6): 865–78.

Waldfogel, Jane. 1998. "Understanding the 'Family Gap' in Pay for Women with Children." *Journal of Economic Perspectives* 12(1): 137–56.

———. 2001. "International Policies toward Parental Leave and Child Care." *Future of Children* 11(1): 99–111.

Wall, Glenda, and Stephanie Arnold. 2007. "How Involved Is Involved Fathering? An Exploration of the Contemporary Culture of Fatherhood." *Gender and Society* 21(4): 508–27.

Walsh, Katherine Cramer. 2010. *Talking about Politics: Informal Groups and Social Identity in American Life.* Chicago: University of Chicago Press.

Wang, Wendy, Kim Parker, and Paul Taylor. 2013. *Breadwinner Moms.* Washington, DC: Pew Research Center. http://www.pewsocialtrends.org/files/2013/05/Breadwinner_moms_final.pdf.

Ward, Kelly Anne, and Lisa Wold-Wendel. 2012. *Academic Motherhood: How Faculty Manage Work and Family.* New Brunswick, NJ: Rutgers University Press.

Weingast, Barry R. 1995. "The Economic Role of Political Institutions: Market-Preserving Federalism and Economic Development." *Journal of Law, Economics, and Organization* 11(1): 1–31.

Laurie Lee Weinstein, and Francine D'Amico. 1999. "Introduction." In *Gender Camouflage: Women and the U.S. Military*, ed. Francine D'Amico and Laurie Lee Weinstein. New York: New York University Press.

Wetherell, Margaret, Stephanie Taylor, and Simeon J. Yates. 2001. *Discourse Theory and Practice: A Reader.* Thousand Oaks, CA: Sage.

Williams, Joan. 2000. *Unbending Gender: Why Family and Work Conflict and What to Do about It.* Oxford: New York: Oxford University Press.

———. 2009. "Reconstructive Feminism: Changing the Way We Talk about Gender and Work Thirty Years after the PDA." *Yale Journal of Law and Feminism* 21:79.

Williams, Joan C., and Holly Cohen Cooper. 2004. "The Public Policy of Motherhood." *Journal of Social Issues* 60(4): 849–65.

Williams, Joan, and Rachel Dempsey. 2014. *What Works for Women at Work: Four Patterns Working Women Need to Know.* New York: New York University Press.

Williams, Mary Elizabeth. 2009. "She Wouldn't Deploy, She Got Arrested." Salon.com.

Williams, Patricia J. 1987. "Alchemical Notes: Reconstructing Ideals from Deconstructed Rights." *Harvard Civil Rights–Civil Liberties Law Review* 22:401.

———. 1991. *Alchemy of Race and Rights: Diary of a Law Professor.* Cambridge, MA: Harvard University Press.

Wolfinger, Nicholas H., Mary Ann Mason, and Marc Goulden. 2009. "Stay in the Game: Gender, Family Formation and Alternative Trajectories in the Academic Life Course." *Social Forces* 87(3): 1591–1621.

Women's Memorial Foundation. "Highlights in the History of Military Women." http://www.womensmemorial.org/Education/timeline.html (accessed October 6, 2016).

World Bank. "Ratio of Female to Male Labor Force Participation Rate." http://data.worldbank.org/indicator/SL.TLF.CACT.FM.ZS (accessed July 8, 2015).

Yamada, David C. 2007. "Dignity, 'Rankism,' and Hierarchy in the Workplace: Creating a 'Dignitarian' Agenda for American Employment Law." *Berkeley Journal of Employment and Labor Law* 28(1): 306–25.

Zellman, Gail L., Susan M. Gates, Joy S. Moini, and Marika Suttorp. 2009. "Meeting Family and Military Needs through Military Child Care." *Armed Forces and Society* 35(3): 437–59.

Zippel, Kathrin. 2004. "Implementing Sexual Harassment Law in the United States and Germany." In *Equality in the Workplace: Gendering Workplace Policy Analysis*, ed. Heidi Gottfried and Laura Reese. 183–214. Lanham, MD: Lexington Books.

Index

academia. *See* public universities
Affordable Care Act, 3
Afghanistan wars, 43–44
Albiston, Catherine, 10, 13–14; on
    ideal worker stereotypes, 118–19;
    on informal institutional net-
    works, 64–65; on informal legal
    literacy, 34
American Association of University
    Women Educational Foundation
    survey, 25
Archer, Emerald, 45
asymmetrical models of equality,
    123–24

breast feeding, 3; in public universi-
    ties, 28; in the U.S. military, 47,
    60, 150n27, 150n32, 152n20
Buck, Catherine L., 45

Calavita, Kitty, 4
career interruption rates, 3
Chen, Julie J., 3
Clinton, Bill, 23
COBRA (Consolidated Omnibus

Budget Reconciliation Act), 30,
    148n24
Connelly, Rachel, 26–27

Daley, Kelly, 130
D'Amico, Francine, 44, 46
Dempsey, Rachel, 3
discursive institutionalism, 83–86,
    95, 98–99, 124–25, 133. *See also*
    rank; workplace discourse
domesticity, 12–13, 104–6, 121, 152n8

Edelman, Lauren B., 62–63
England, Lynndie, 44, 148n4
Enloe, Cynthia, 106
Epp, Charles, 133–34
equality in the workplace, 15–16,
    122–39; feminist theory on,
    123–24; ideal worker norms and,
    125–27, 138; legal limitations of,
    127–33; potential solutions for,
    133–37, 154n22, 154n24; women of
    higher rank and, 124–26
Evans, Elrina, 148n21
Ewick, Patricia, 5, 11, 65

39; equality in the workplace and, 15–16, 122–27; legal parameters of, 2–3, 14–15, 127–33; potential solutions for, 133–37, 154n22, 154n24; public policy and, 102–3, 118–23; scholarly study of, 16–17. *See also* family leave policies

workplace discourse, 133–39; institutional support of, 136–39; training of institutional leaders and, 134–35